Like Dragons Did They Fight

The Sons of Helaman™

Methods of Fighting Addictions
And Other Psychological, Spiritual, Emotional and
Bio-chemical Battles

By Maurice W. Harker, CMHC
With
Lucas J. Reynolds

Revised 10/9/2014

Like Dragons Did They Fight

Printed in the United States of America

ISBN 978-1-105-94797-1

Life Changing Services, Inc.
722 Shepard Lane, Ste. 105
Farmington, Utah 84025
1-877-HERO-877

Visit us at www.lifechangingservices.org.

"But they fought for their lives,
and for their wives,
and for their children;
therefore they exerted themselves
*and **like dragons did they fight**."*

Mosiah 20:11

Testimonials

"As a priesthood leader I have referred members to a number of different mental health professionals. For the past several years I have narrowed the number of those professionals to primarily one: Maurice Harker. His research and understanding of sexual addiction is better than any other therapist I have ever met. His methods and counseling (including the Sons of Helaman youth groups) are superior to any I've experienced. His success rates at helping people overcome addiction and transgression have been remarkable. I can't give a high enough recommendation for Maurice Harker as a counselor and therapist."

--President Thomas V. Beard, Stake President, Kaysville Crestwood Stake

"I am glad that I found the Sons of Helaman program. It's made me the man I have become today. I am now home from a mission and I am temple worthy; I like who I have become. I know that anyone who follows what they have learned in this program will succeed. The Sons of Helaman gave me the knowledge that Satan is real and he is doing his best to ruin my life. Also, and more importantly, God became real to me as well as my Savior Jesus Christ—I know they exist. I know they love and care about me and who I become in this life."

--C. F., Graduate of the Sons of Helaman Program

"First, I would like to say that this problem truly is a fight, and it will take time to overcome, but the rewards are so worth it. Becoming free will change your life and the lives of those around you for the best. Through this program and the guidance of your peers, you will discover strength in yourself and deeper faith in the Lord. I wish you well, and hope for the best."

--Chris, Graduate of the Sons of Helaman Program

"I find the Sons of Helaman program to be a remarkably effective treatment for young men struggling with pornography addiction. Maurice Harker has discovered a powerful key - that adolescent & young adult males respond best when they are in a TEAM environment, and as members of a team they often find the courage to confront & overcome these powerful temptations. They learn that they are bigger than the Temptation after all!"

--Larry Lewis, CMHC, author of *Receive Ye One Another*

Acknowledgements

First I want to thank my wife. She has been the primary stimulant of my inspiration and insight. She has been a guiding light to me. She has been my most accurate sounding board. She has been patient with me as I have taken time from the family to complete these writings. I would not have grown into the man I am today without her.

When I write, I tend to dive deep into a topic, and then I jump randomly to a completely unrelated topic. Lucas Reynolds has saved the day by reading through hundreds of clips of my writings and bringing together the relevant pieces into a cohesive narrative. Also, he has sat in on many of the Sons of Helaman group sessions and has written up many pieces that filled in the gaps. He is very insightful and an excellent student.

My executive secretary, Aneladee Milne, has not only successfully and pleasantly pressured me into completing this book, but she has orchestrated events behind the scenes to help facilitate the practicalities of getting the book published. She has taken the load off my shoulders in many other areas, thus allowing me time and mental space to write.

I wish to thank Lisa Peterson for her editing skills. It appears that I am like every other author who does not see the errors in his own writings. I thank her for eliminating all the embarrassing flaws in my writing.

And finally, I want to thank the young warriors with whom I have learned so much as we stand shoulder to shoulder these many years, learning and fighting as we go. I am so deeply edified by their strong spirits. They have inspired me to work and teach and learn and write. I just pray that the information found in this book will give back to them and all the warriors to come.

Maurice W. Harker

Author's Note

Dear Reader,

I have put my heart and soul into the information you are about to read. The agony I have felt for those who have become slaves to addiction has driven me to provide effective information and services. Even so, there is always the possibility of missing something that might matter to you. If at any time you have a question about or a request for clarification on the topics addressed in this book, please email them to me at:

mwharkertherapy@gmail.com

If the answer to your question(s) will benefit all readers, I will include my response on my blog: mwharkertherapist.blogspot.com. Otherwise, you can expect a personal response if you include a return email address. I add to my blog regularly. I recommend visiting it often as I there delve deeper into becoming free from addiction and strengthening relationships.

Enjoy your reading. I felt inspired as I discovered the amazing principles that I now give to you. I hope you feel equally inspired as you read them.

Your Devoted Servant,

Maurice W. Harker

Table of Contents

Acknowledgements

First I want to thank my wife. She has been the primary stimulant of my inspiration and insight. She has been a guiding light to me. She has been my most accurate sounding board. She has been patient with me as I have taken time from the family to complete these writings. I would not have grown into the man I am today without her.

When I write, I tend to dive deep into a topic, and then I jump randomly to a completely unrelated topic. Lucas Reynolds has saved the day by reading through hundreds of clips of my writings and bringing together the relevant pieces into a cohesive narrative. Also, he has sat in on many of the Sons of Helaman group sessions and has written up many pieces that filled in the gaps. He is very insightful and an excellent student.

My executive secretary, Aneladee Milne, has not only successfully and pleasantly pressured me into completing this book, but she has orchestrated events behind the scenes to help facilitate the practicalities of getting the book published. She has taken the load off my shoulders in many other areas, thus allowing me time and mental space to write.

I wish to thank Lisa Peterson for her editing skills. It appears that I am like every other author who does not see the errors in his own writings. I thank her for eliminating all the embarrassing flaws in my writing.

And finally, I want to thank the young warriors with whom I have learned so much as we stand shoulder to shoulder these many years, learning and fighting as we go. I am so deeply edified by their strong spirits. They have inspired me to work and teach and learn and write. I just pray that the information found in this book will give back to them and all the warriors to come.

Maurice W. Harker

Author's Note

Dear Reader,

I have put my heart and soul into the information you are about to read. The agony I have felt for those who have become slaves to addiction has driven me to provide effective information and services. Even so, there is always the possibility of missing something that might matter to you. If at any time you have a question about or a request for clarification on the topics addressed in this book, please email them to me at:

mwharkertherapy@gmail.com

If the answer to your question(s) will benefit all readers, I will include my response on my blog: mwharkertherapist.blogspot.com. Otherwise, you can expect a personal response if you include a return email address. I add to my blog regularly. I recommend visiting it often as I there delve deeper into becoming free from addiction and strengthening relationships.

Enjoy your reading. I felt inspired as I discovered the amazing principles that I now give to you. I hope you feel equally inspired as you read them.

Your Devoted Servant,

Maurice W. Harker

PART 1
The Problem

Chapter 1

The Pain

You have tried everything. You are not stupid. You have decent self-discipline in almost all other areas of your life. You know better. It is not like someone has to motivate you to stop your misbehaviors. You have hated it from the beginning...and still...it comes back again, and again, and again. It is almost impossible to talk to anyone about it. No one is going to understand. They are just going to tell you what you already know – it is bad to do and you should stop or you are going to "Hell".

For a while you maintained hope. You have succeeded before in other things, you can succeed again. You have been a problem solver and you will solve this one also. But...it's not working this time. You have begun withdrawing from those who will be disappointed. You have begun crossing things off your list of goals for your future – like serving a mission and getting married in the temple. You might be questioning your faith, or looking for ways to find fault in what you've always known and accepted to be true. You may also think that there's something fundamentally wrong with you, that you are defective, cursed, or must have been bad in the pre-existence. You could lie about your struggles – so many others do and get away with it. You have lied before, and it only made things worse. Now, you just avoid those who will be disappointed and/or judgmental. You catch yourself doing things to get others to leave you alone.

You find yourself identifying with the man in the New Testament (see Mark 9:17-29) who had already tried everything in hopes of finding a solution for his son's illness, and nothing was working. Christ was not intimidated by the previous lack of success. He first recognized that there was a Dark Spiritual Element involved in torturing the young man. After the father begged for compassion, "Jesus said unto him, 'If thou canst believe, all things are possible to him that believeth.'" Not surprisingly, "the father of the child cried out, and said with tears, Lord, I believe; help thou mine unbelief."

The problems this young man was dealing with were resolved by prayer and fasting. I am going to guess that you have already tried that. Two thousand years after this event, Satan has improved and diversified his fighting weapons. He has become really, *really,* good at what he does. He has had thousands of years of practice, and billions of people to practice on. You've had only a few years, and only yourself to work on. Whether you realize it or not, you are in the fight of your life, and the enemy you're fighting uses weapons unknown to you. In this day and age, prayer, fasting, thought control and exercise are often not enough.

But we do not have to give up. The Gospel of Jesus Christ is the source of all truth. In it we find answers on how to beat Satan, even when he uses his most "state-of-the-art" diabolical methods of attempting to destroy our lives. In many of the Book of Mormon stories, along with the power of God, the warriors had to use their bodies, the ferocity of dragons (Mosiah 20:11), and "stratagem" to defeat their enemies (Alma 43:30). The warrior will need to learn to use a combination of body and spirit weapons and methods if he is going to win this war.

We are told over and over again that "God...will not suffer you to be tempted above that ye are able" So, many conclude that if they are still losing battles, it is because of some kind of personal weakness. I have found quite the opposite. It is important to read the rest of 1 Corinthians 10:13, "but will with the temptation also make a way to escape". In some stories from the scriptures, like when the Israelites were enslaved by the Egyptians for a very long time before a way was provided for them to escape, if you have been enslaved by an addiction, it may take time and training at a whole new level in order to escape.

I am sad that what you have tried so far has not worked. My awareness of your pain is what drives me to write this book. We now have a much greater understanding of Satan's modern war tactics. After years of "reconnaissance" and "battle-tested" experience, I am pleased to report that we now know how to beat him. It takes training, education and practice. But if you are determined, it can be done. As the Prophet Joseph Smith said, "All beings who have bodies have power over those who have not. The devil has no power over us only as we permit him" (*Teachings of Presidents of the Church: Joseph Smith* (2007), 214).

I invite you to risk hoping again. I invite you to shed humiliation and hopelessness. I invite you to learn how to fight in a way that will actually work! I invite you to read on.

Chapter 2

The Attack

(From within the mind of Satan)

"It's not too late! I can still beat God. I can win the war. I need to start by identifying those who are most likely to be leaders of the next generation, and then I will wipe them out! I remember that in the times of Moses and of Christ, I was able to persuade the political leaders of their times to commit mass infanticide, having all the 2 year olds killed in an attempt to take out the prime individuals who I feared would rise up and cause serious problems for me. That strategy didn't work. Anyway, in today's society, political leaders are not willing to commit political suicide. I need to fine tune my methods of destruction. I have learned a great deal about mortal psychology over the last 7,000 years. I believe I can now truly be 'the serpent [who is] more subtle than any beast of the field' (Gen. 3:1).

"I will start by attacking them before they are old enough to fight back. I know that is unsportsmanlike of me, but I don't care. I have observed that even though young men do not reach the age of puberty until early to mid-teens, their bodies still have a chemical reaction to 'opportunities to reproduce.' I will use the modern technology of internet and cell phones combined with the impulsiveness of youth to have them pass these images on to one another as fast as possible. Most of the young men who experience these chemical reactions will enjoy it so much that they will ignore any whispers of 'this is the wrong time and wrong place to be feeling this' sensations. They will easily slip into becoming addicted to the chemicals. But these are not the ones I am really after.

"I am after the Warriors, the ones who are driven to 'become someone' or 'do important things with their lives'. Adults around them have taught them and they are on the verge of 'knowing who they are.' These are the ones that I must target with great intensity or all will be lost. So, here is what I will do. I will have the calloused ones—people who are deaf to the voice of the Holy Ghost—throw images at these valiant young warriors and mock any attempt at self-defense. Or, I can use modern technology to hit them when they least expect it. I can easily convince them that 'once more won't hurt' and that 'no one will find out'. I can get them to allow themselves a handful of exposures to 'opportunities to reproduce' until they experience enough brain chemical reactions that they become addicts. Glorious!!! It has begun. Once this has happened, the seeds are planted.

"I, Satan, have learned from scientists that the chemicals associated with this experience are a fascinating combination of stimulants and soothing agents. Some scientists have compared it to heroin. During the formative years, as the young man transitions into adolescence, the pain and frustrations of being a teenager become profound. Whenever he is experiencing this pain at 'intolerable levels', I can suggest the need for 'soothing'. This pain can come in so many entertaining forms! There is fear, loneliness, anxiety, depression, hopelessness, feeling overwhelmed, to name only a few. I have also learned that each of these feelings comes with its own chemical reactions inside the human brain, separate from the 'deviant' chemicals. The chemical reactions associated with strong emotions can create the sensation of spinning out of control. For example, with anxiety I can throw ideas into their heads like, 'You are never going to get it all done. You are going to run out of time. They are not going to like you anyway.' Each of these primary emotions can be stimulated to the point of real pain.

"I have learned from more scientists, that a certain part of the brain is designed to keep track of effective (short term) ways to decrease emotional pain. If, while in the prematuration phase of life, the youth's brain discovered the powerfully soothing chemicals associated with 'opportunities to reproduce', they will quickly get the idea to 'use' again. If I manipulate the chemicals gradually enough, they won't even notice the frontal lobe (values system) and cerebral cortex (creative problem solving) parts of their brain shutting down. I can help bring to their awareness the steps they need to take in order to 'use' again.

"Once the activity is over, these chemicals will quickly drain out of the blood stream. The mental energy returns to the frontal lobe and the cerebral cortex and the young man feels very unintelligent. This is so much fun for me because I know that for these Warriors – of any age – the need to feel confident and competent is very strong. They ask the question, 'Why did I do that?' They assume, since they cannot see any outside cause of the problem, that *they* must be the problem. When I can set up a scenario where they feel dumb and out of control, they gradually lose all sense of manhood.

"The adolescent years are the formative years for identity. I want to arrange for them to go through this cycle many times. Each time they can't figure out what is happening. If I can get them to start to believe that there really is something wrong with them, eventually, they will start to lose hope. They don't want to feel even more incompetent by asking for help. Gradually, they start to reject even those who love them most. They give up on the future. They allow themselves to slide into lives of 'quiet desperation' – no longer a threat – no longer desiring to become what they were predestined to become.

"In Doctrine and Covenants section 138, verses 55-56, it reads:

'I observed that they were also among the noble and great ones who were chosen in the beginning to be rulers in the Church of God.

'Even before they were born, they, with many others, received their first lessons in the world of spirits and were prepared to come forth in the due time of the Lord to labor in his vineyard for the salvation of the souls of men.'

"God wants them to labor in His vineyard for the salvation of souls; but, instead, they will become my brainless slaves…forever!"

Chapter 3

A Parable

Why are They Losing Battles?

When this "vision" of the mind of Satan first started to become clear to me, I was left in a state of shock and fear. The more I learned, the more hopeless I felt. An unseen and extremely intelligent enemy is using scientific means to neutralize the most powerful men of the coming generation!

It was a great blessing to remember the phrase from the Old Testament, "Those that be with us are more than those that be with them" (2 Kings 6:1-6).

The question I asked basically was "Why do smart people do stupid things?" Youth and adults that are so disciplined and capable in other areas of their lives can still find themselves struggling with these terrible addictions. Why is that? Understanding the answer to these questions begins by understanding true psychology—what the word psychology literally means.

"Psychology" by definition means: psych = "spirit"; ology = "the study of." Putting the two pieces together it means, "the study of the spirit." Unfortunately, many of my fellow professionals have neglected the spiritual side of understanding addictions. Ignoring man's spirit, and the Creator of man's spirit, they unsuccessfully try to find solutions to problems like addiction that plague the human race.

I am convinced that men are by nature good. Because of who we were spiritually before we were born, we have a natural tendency to do good. The only time we do things that are destructive, either to ourselves or to our relationships, is when such behaviors are initiated by an intelligent, skilled, destructive spiritual entity. In our culture, we call this entity, Satan.

We have learned that Satan is a military strategist. One intelligent element in the strategy for winning a war is to take out the opposing leaders. The young men he targets these days tend to have one thing in common; they are each a major threat to Satan. They are on their way to becoming important contributors and leaders in this world.

Satan has learned that if you are going to wipe out future leaders you need to do so while they are still young; not yet able to fight back. And, instead of trying to kill them physically, he works to enslave them to addictive chemicals in their youth. He has learned that the military strategies used by the British in the Revolutionary War were too obvious and easy to defend. Direct and obvious temptation does not work on these modern, valiant warriors. So when he wants to "tempt" a young man to engage in misbehaviors, he has worked to become "the most subtle of all the beasts of the field." Satan went through a phase of using psychological tactics similar to that which you would find in the Vietnam War: Guerilla Warfare. By sneaking around in the shadows of our minds and our technology, many have been snared.

That was 40 years ago. Since then, Satan has advanced his strategies to an even more devious level. I will use one of my fictional tales to illustrate these most recent advancements in Satanic Warfare. This imaginary story takes place somewhere in the middle of the Book of Mormon.

Lamanites vs. Nephites

The Lamanites return to their camp from another battle with the Nephites having lost again. The leader hangs his head in shame while the followers whine and complain. Yet, once again, they raise their fists and swear oaths that they will win next time, although they have no idea how.

While they are all sitting around, one of the more nerdy Lamanites (you know, the one wearing a pocket protector and quirky glasses and his loin-cloth hiked up to his rib cage) comes rushing out of the forest and into the camp. He approaches the leader of the Lamanite army with great hope and enthusiasm. He is a member of the research and development team.

"Oh Great Leader, while exploring in the forest I found this really cool plant. If we dry the leaves and grind them into powder, then sprinkle the powder into the water source of the Nephites, we can get them all stoned!"

It doesn't take long for the Leader to catch the vision. He takes a team of men and they find the stream that delivers clean drinking water into the Nephite city. Every day they sprinkle some of the intoxicating powder into the water of the Nephites. Not too much though; they don't want the Nephites to notice!

In the meantime, Captain Moroni is down in the Nephite city fine tuning the strength and skills of his men. They are doing push-ups and sit ups. They are drilling with swords, knives, shields, bows and arrows. They are running laps. And...drinking the water.... Because there is so little of the powder in the water, they are unable to recognize its presence.

After 5 days or so, the Lamanites, who have been anxiously waiting with weapons of war in hand, rush toward the Nephite city with a blood-curdling yell. Captain Moroni sees them coming and calls out to his men, "Charge!" He is horrified when he looks behind himself and finds his men of great valor can barely stand on their own two feet. What is going to happen to his men if he sends them into battle in this condition? Even worse, what is going to happen to their women and children if they don't fight?

The Lamanites begin to slaughter the Nephite armies. Captain Moroni calls out, "Gentlemen, fight harder!" anxious to save his men. This doesn't work. "Gentlemen, fight smarter!" This doesn't work either. "Sing a hymn?! Recite a scripture?!" He calls out with dwindling hope. Imagine how this battle is going to end. Imagine being one of these warriors who has trained his whole life to fight for things he cares about only to find himself unable to use the skills and weapons he has worked so hard to develop.

Let's come back to current reality for a moment. Similar to the story above, Satan has found a way to trigger the brain chemistry of good, solid men, both young and old; similar to the way the Lamanites drugged the Nephites in the story above. These modern warriors are often very disciplined and faithful in every other aspect of life, yet find themselves slipping into addictive behaviors to a destructive level.

The following is the story of one of my clients; we'll call this young man Jim.

I met Jim as a newly-returned missionary, still getting used to normal life. Jim had been a good, faithful LDS Missionary and had loved serving the Lord with all his heart, might, mind and strength. He was obedient to the rules, successful, well-liked by his fellow missionaries, and a leader in his mission.

Before getting called on his mission, Jim had struggled with unwanted pornography and masturbation behaviors, but working with his Bishop had conquered this problem and he had moved forward. He prepared worthily for a mission, and couldn't have been more content than in the service of His Savior.

Then, something completely unexpected happened. One day, out of the blue it seemed, Jim's addictive behaviors returned. He didn't know how the unwanted behavior had re-infiltrated his life. He felt embarrassed and ashamed. How could he be a representative of the Lord, and a leader in the mission field, and be committing such a "bad" sin? He felt alone and went to his mission president to confess and ask for help.

During the rest of his mission, Jim struggled with the addiction. How could he be so obedient and faithful in every other aspect of the work, and yet feel completely out of control in this very embarrassing way? He was being chemically altered and he didn't even know it.

After his return home, Jim's bishop recommended that he come see me, and shortly afterwards we were sitting across from each other in my office. When I explained the analogy of Captain Moroni and the drugged soldiers his eyes lit up: "You mean that explains why I could be so good in so many areas, and just never seem to get this under control?"

"That is exactly why."

In the next chapter I will give a description of how the scientific and the spiritual worlds intersect so you can understand what happens inside the mind of a "drugged" warrior.

Chapter 4

The Satanic Spin™

Being an addict can feel very out-of-control. It can feel like a downward, hopeless spiral. Here are the words of one client. If you've struggled with addictions, this might sound familiar:

"I cannot describe how it happened. A few minutes before, I thought everything was normal; now my head hangs in shame. I just lost another battle. I hate this. No matter how hard I try, I can be doing great spiritually or emotionally, and then WHAM! It is like I am hit by a two-by-four, knocking me into the ditch. I find myself totally out of control. My life seems to be going normally, and then a random thought will enter, but for some reason I don't have the strength to fight it. I know I shouldn't dwell on the temptation, but I feel frozen. Life seems to be in slow motion. *You need to stop!* I tell myself. *I will…in just a second.* Before I know it the battle is over and I feel stupid. Why is this happening to me?"

So, "Why do smart people do stupid things?" I have found that the answer is simple. Satan is an expert tempter and has found how to use human psychology to manipulate good men and women to break all the rules they would, under normal circumstances, value above everything else. Refer to the diagram on the following page as I explain this process.

When people with addictions describe what they experience before a "lost battle," a common pattern is revealed, a spin, resembling a downward spiral. They describe it as if they are unknowingly being drugged. I have discovered four elements to this Spin, each element feeding off the others. There is a gradual acceleration and loss of control which finally culminates in the addict engaging in behavior contrary to their personal values. Sadly, the scientific sophistication of this drift validates to me the existence of a cunning adversary who has refined his strategies for over 7,000 years!

Before I proceed, I will add a quick disclaimer: I have spent my professional career simplifying complex psychological concepts, so they are easily understood by the layman, especially teenagers. The concepts behind what you are about to read are scientifically sound. Please learn from the principles and you will find they resonate.

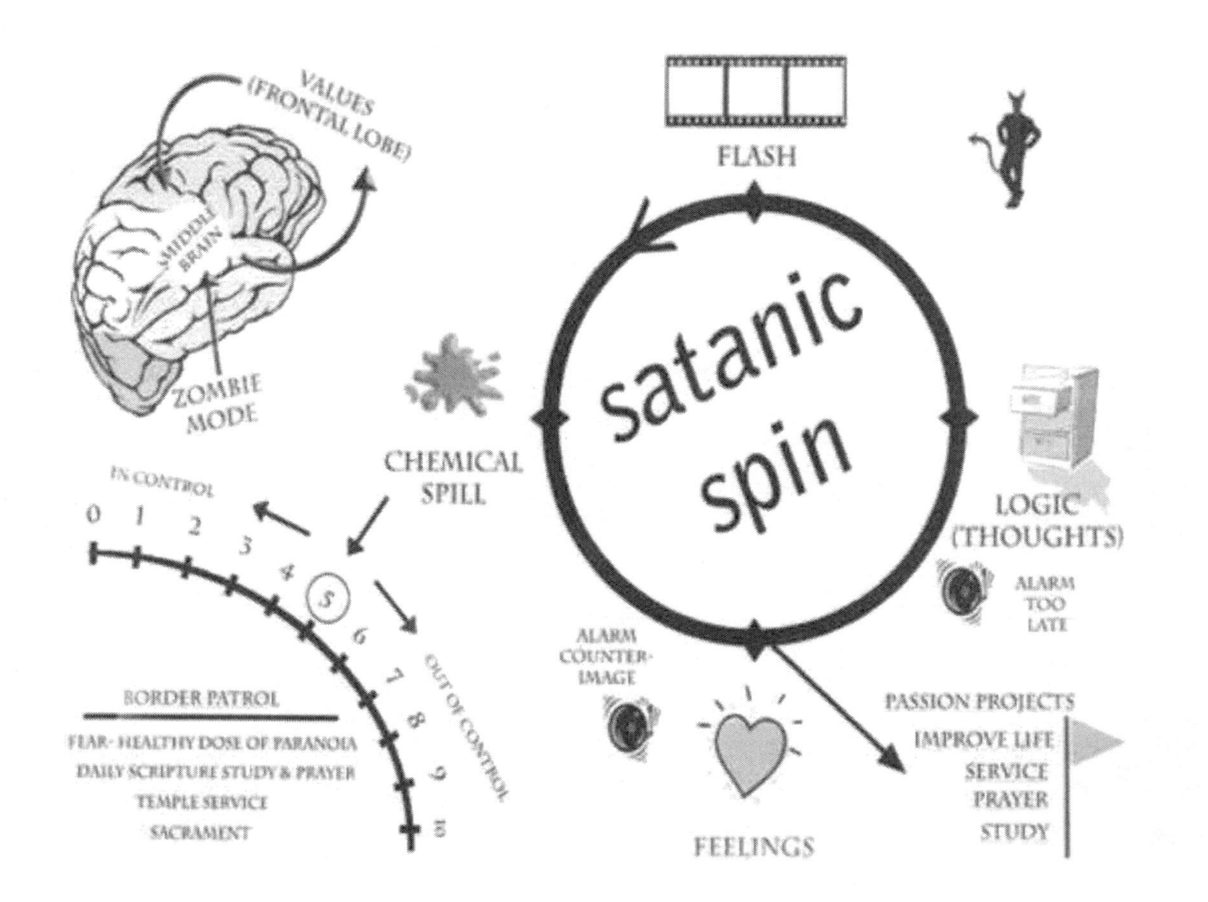
VALUES
(FRONTAL LOBE)
MIDDLE BRAIN
ZOMBIE
MODE
FLASH
satanic
spin
CHEMICAL
SPILL
LOGIC
(THOUGHTS)
ALARM
TOO
LATE
ALARM
COUNTER-
IMAGE
FEELINGS
PASSION PROJECTS
IMPROVE LIFE
SERVICE
PRAYER
STUDY
IN CONTROL
0 1 2 3 4 5 6 7 8 9 10
OUT OF CONTROL
BORDER PATROL
FEAR- HEALTHY DOSE OF PARANOIA
DAILY SCRIPTURE STUDY & PRAYER
TEMPLE SERVICE
SACRAMENT

1. The Flash – About 40 years ago a marketing company began an experiment in movie theaters. They cut out one frame of a film and inserted an advertisement in its place. As the movie quickly scrolled by (about 24 squares per second), the conscious brain overlooked the image, but the subconscious mind captured the idea. Preconditioned members of the audience were stimulated with an irresistible urge to purchase the advertised product. The experiment was so dangerously successful it was eventually outlawed.

In my office, I ask my clients to quietly listen for the sound of the ticking clock. Within seconds they hear the ticking and over the next few moments, the volume seems to grow louder. I explain that the ticking does not actually grow louder; in fact, our brains have been registering the ticking sound the entire time. We, however, don't consciously *notice* it. This lends the question, "Are there other ideas being thrown at our minds, as fast as the movie theater frame and as quiet as the ticking of the clock?"

As do most Christians, we believe in inspiration. By definition it is the experience of having positive, motivating thoughts enter our minds from an external or Divine source, the Holy Ghost. Though not commonly discussed, we also believe Satan has similar power. Satan is able to insert ideas, pictures, thoughts, even full DVDs of information into our minds. It is very uncomfortable to discover that the most "subtle" of all the beasts of the field has learned how to throw ideas into our minds as fast as the movie theater flash and as quietly as the ticking of the clock. If such thoughts had as little influence as a ticking clock, the results would not be so devastating.

He complicates things by speaking to us in our own voice. It shocked me when I learned he could do this. When he combines my voice with highly logical thoughts, I have learned that I can only catch him (discern his presence) by the way he feels, or more specifically, the way I feel when he speaks to me.

2. *The Chemical Spill* – Many have experienced driving a vehicle and seeing flashing lights in their rearview mirror. After the eye captures the image of the police car, the mind registers the meaning of the lights and sends a signal to the adrenal glands, releasing adrenaline into the bloodstream. This entire process takes less than one second. Even if the officer pulls past your car, it takes approximately 15 – 30 minutes for the body's natural filtering systems to clean the chemicals out of the blood stream. In the meantime, the body continues having a noticeable physical reaction to the chemicals.

Now let's alter our story. You are back in the car, but this time in the passenger seat there is a man from a remote tribe in Africa, who has never seen a car, a road, or a police officer. Does he have the same adrenal reaction that you had? No! Why? *Because it is not the flashing lights that cause the adrenaline dump, it is the thought of what the flashing lights represent that triggers the chemical reaction.*

In other words, certain thoughts can cause chemical reactions in the brain. Unfortunately, Satan has also figured this out. Satan cannot read one's mind but, after 7,000 years, he has honed his skill of guessing what ideas ("Flashes") will cause chemical reactions in an individual's body. With sexual addiction, his objective is for a release of what I call Deviant Sex Chemicals™. Unfortunately as a precursor, he works to manipulate other brain chemical dynamics, with the intent to increase negative emotions such as anxiety, depression, and boredom. These additional chemical reactions have a strong tendency to inhibit our resolve to fight off the deviant chemicals. Researchers are discovering that these chemicals are in the same family as heroin.

3. Partial Feelings/Emotions – One thing that makes humans unique from computers is that body chemistry changes affect how one feels. We typically don't notice chemical changes in our bodies (especially men), but we can, with some effort and training, identify changes in feelings and emotions. This is foreign to most men. When trained to recognize subtle changes in body chemistry, one often describes it using the following words: antsy, bored, irritable, frustrated, curious, anxious, depressed, lonely, angry, bugged, or deviant. Imagine that in your brain many little buckets exist, filled with chemicals. When these buckets are spilled, they can create a myriad of unique feelings. When Satan identifies a young man as valiant and capable and he realizes that the Red Coat and the Vietnam strategies won't work, he turns to Chemical Warfare. He looks for an idea that will tip a bucket just enough to create a slight change in feelings. A full chemical dump is too easy to perceive, thus a slight spill is preferred. He does not want the victim to have a full awareness of what is going on.

4. ***Filing Cabinets*** – The human brain stores memories of everything you have ever seen, tasted, touched, smelled, felt or experienced in any way. When you see a previous acquaintance that you cannot identify because of an incomplete memory, your brain begins asking, "Where have I seen this person before?" This process happens many times per second in an effort to remember. Similarly, when a single drop of chemical is spilled in the brain, it creates an incomplete set of feelings. When this happens, your brain asks many times per second, "Where have I f[illegible] this sensation before?" The brain abhors the discomfort of an unsolved puzzle, so it keeps searching its files until it remembers a time when it had a similar feeling. A memory is found in the filing cabinets and instantly flashes in the mind, becoming the next "Flash" and the spin continues. A second role of chemicals in the brain is to tell the brain in which area to heighten functioning and in which area to decrease functioning. As these uncomfortable and painful emotions build, the energy of the brain vacates the values part of the brain (frontal lobe) and the creative problem solving part of the brain (cerebral cortex). The build-up of uncomfortable emotions masks the undercurrent of increasing deviant chemicals. These two combined create the sensation of being "stoned". By the time the individual notices the invitation (thought) to do something against their value system, the will-power to fight against it has been lost. The frontal lobe is asleep and the mid-brain is ready to go. Conscious decision making has come to an end. Satan holds his hands up and innocently says, "What? I wasn't even there. It was your own choice to do something like that. There must be something wrong with you. You can't even control yourself. What makes you think you will ever be useful? Give up on being a future leader!"

Spinning - The human brain processes this entire four-phase cycle in less than one second.

With every cycle, strong negative (painful) feelings are intensified in one direction, while deviant chemicals sooth the mind to the point of being "stoned".

Chapter 5

The Chemical Scale™

In order to fight back, the warrior will need to know how "stoned" they are. The Chemical Scale ranges from zero to ten (see diagram). It is intentionally shaped like the edge of a whirlpool. An addict can identify how stoned he is by where he falls on the scale. It is best understood by counting backward from:

10 – Crash. This is self-explanatory. The addict has a lost battle. By lost battle, we mean any behavior that is contrary to your values system.

6-9 – The Fall. We don't talk much about this phase because there is not much to talk about. The addict is spiraling.

5 – The "I Give Up" moment. This is the moment in time when the individual stops fighting the temptation (this time). His ability to hold on to his values system is exhausted. This is what I call the Action Stage.

4 – The Irrational Conversation. "You know where this is headed." "Yeah, I know." "Probably should stop." "Yeah, I know, I will...in a minute...." This conversation or something like it is very familiar to addicts. It is part of the journey to level 5 and ultimately to level 10. This is what I call the Words Stage.

3 – The "Dude" moment. This is the first moment that the individual notices the thought to do something inappropriate. "Dude, your parents aren't home." "Dude, it's been a while." "Dude, it will make you feel better." Text books call this the "trigger" moment. Religion calls it the "temptation" moment. Men tend to be *thought* oriented, so this tends to be the first stage of the Chemical Scale they recognize. Unfortunately the individual has already gone through two levels of increased chemicals *before they even notice* what is happening to them. Now there are 30ish drops of heroin type chemicals. This is what I call the Thoughts Stage.

2 – Feelings Stage. Before the thought of doing something that is against your Values System is thrown into your mind at a noticeable level, Satan has to knock you off balance using emotional pain. "Yeah, but this time I have a really good reason to feel this way." Whether your Achilles' heel feeling is anxiety, depression, self-loathing, frustration, feeling overwhelmed, irritation, or any other negative emotion, Satan will flash thoughts into your head that are true, or mostly true, just for the purpose of altering your brain chemistry. All of these negative emotions are associated with chemical reactions in the brain that start to drain the upper regions of the brain and move the energy toward the animal (survival) brain. As the panic increases, the willingness to "do whatever it takes to be relieved" increases, and attachment to one's Values System decreases.

Deviant chemicals often carry a type of pain relieving sensation. In order to get the brain to accommodate the pain reliever, it needs to experience the pain. Prior to reaching Level 3, the dominant feelings the addict experiences are the painful, negative emotions as indicated in section 3 of the Satanic Spin model. Under the surface, deviant chemicals build. By the time the individual notices the invitation to betray his value system, he is too "stoned" to do anything about it. He has 10 more drops of "heroin" in his system.

1 – Chemicals. For the purpose of explanation, it takes about 10 laps around the Satanic Spin to get to a Level 1. This means the warrior has about 10 drops of a heroin type substance in their brains at this point. You don't hear people saying things like, "Hey, I think I am having a slight brain chemistry change right now." Why? Because they don't notice it. The initial spins are so subtle; the untrained addict does not recognize them until it is too late. To help a warrior understand what a level 1 feels like, it helps to know what level 0 feels like. When a person is at level 0, or in other words, when they are at their best and are not experiencing any Satanic distortion, then they feel awesome! They are in the mood to do good. They want to serve other people. They want to do well in music, sports, family relations, education. At Level 0, they are in their true, spiritually natural state. Level 1 is when they are a little "off". This when they are not in the mood to do good. They, "don't feel like it." The sensation of "laziness" starts to creep in. Some who spend a great deal of time at level 1 even start to classify themselves as "Lazy", having no idea that they are under attack, in a very subtle way.

As you might guess, the goal is for each of us to function at Level 0 as much as possible. I believe it was Winston Churchill who said, "The only thing Evil needs to win is for Good to do nothing." We are the great warriors of the final generation! We are the Noble and Great Ones. If all the dark side has to do to keep us from our predestination is to keep us at Level 1, where we "don't feel like it", then the war is won, but not by us. I hope by now, after reading about this amazingly subtle attack on your mind and on your life, you are beginning to become ferociously determined to learn how to win!

Part II
The Solution

Chapter 6

Warrior Chemistry™

What Has Not Worked

To understand what battle plans work in fighting Satan, we need to first understand which strategies do not work. Historically, in the field of psychology, the solution to these addictions has been "thought control". The basis of this intervention is that when an individual has deviant thoughts, he should simply kick them out and replace them with constructive thoughts. This may be effective for someone who is not an addict; however, it lacks effectiveness for someone who is addicted and has a pattern of losing control of their body chemistry.

From a spiritual perspective, the use of "thought control" underestimates the power of Satan. Satan's primary weapon is his ability to affect our thought process. It is unwise to pit a person with less than 100 years of experience in a thought control battle against Satan's 7,000 years of practice.

It would be nice to stop the Satanic Flashes, but we learn in LDS scripture that God allows us to be enticed by both good and evil. This part of the spin cannot be eliminated. I often ask the question, "When will the Lamanites stop attacking the Nephites?" The sobering answer is, "When the Nephites are all dead."

It would be nice to disconnect the flashes from the chemical spills, but even when we are able to disconnect a flash from a chemical spill, Satan simply finds new flashes.

Referring back to the Chemical Scale and the Satanic Spin, before the individual identifies they are under attack and becomes aware of their thoughts, they are already at level three. This means they are already under the influence of several chemicals. It is like asking a drunken man to concentrate on driving his vehicle and to stop swerving outside the yellow lines. It is common for both drunks and addicts to believe they have control of their minds, when in reality they do not because they are "under the influence". A drunk may drive in what he thinks is a straight line, and an addict will act in what he thinks is a logical and rational manner.

What Does Work!

Since thought control is ineffective for the addict, what *will* work? Everything I found in text books referred me to thought control. Nowhere was found any acknowledgment of a spiritual element in this war. As I mentioned before, the word psychology means the study of the spirit, if this is really true, I wondered, then shouldn't there be some connection between the spirit and my body chemicals?

After many long hours poring over psychology books for the answers, there appeared to be no solution. Then I remembered a scripture I had heard many times: "If any of you lack wisdom, let him ask of God." (James 1:5) I learned during the first three years of my study of psychology that God is a good psychologist. As I read my text books and asked Him to clarify the principles, I realized how smart He really is!

After laboring through a period of time where I struggled for answers, God responded with a thought I had had before, "You are making it too complicated." Next came the thought; "What do you have that Satan does not have?" After several inaccurate, overly complicated responses, I finally thought, "A body!" He confirmed, "You are right!" I thought, "But that seems to be the problem!" He answered, "Go back to your textbooks and find out why your body is the answer."

As I referred back to my text books, I remembered "all things are created both temporally and spiritually." Temporal can mean "of the body". I remembered from a chemistry class that certain chemicals neutralize each other. Going back to the Lamanite/Nephite story, everything would have been completely different if before the Lamanites arrived at the city, one of Captain Moroni's scientists discovered a different plant which would neutralize the Lamanite drug. With the drugs neutralized, the Nephite warriors would not have to be retrained; they would regain their strength and their values! The Nephites would surprise the Lamanites and continue in dominance!

After understanding this vision, my quest became to find how to release the chemicals in the brain that would counter the deviant chemicals. What were these chemicals, and how do we activate them? I felt great relief when I found that there is a way to counteract the drugging chemicals with which Satan attacks us. I call this counter-chemical, "Warrior Chemistry".

Warrior Chemistry

The best way to understand Warrior Chemistry is to experience it.

Imagine, on a Friday afternoon, after a long week at work, you get a phone call from your wife. She says, "I have made arrangements for the kids tonight, we are going to have an empty house. I would like to have a stay-at-home date night with you." You are no dummy. You know what that means. You find a way to get out of work early so you can pick up flowers, take-out, and a video.

As you pull up to your house, you try not to squeal your tires with enthusiasm. As you move toward the front door, you try not to prance like a ballerina! ☺ As you approach the front door, you find that the door is already 6 inches open. That's strange....

As you push the door open, you hear your wife screaming. As you enter, you see a guy in a ski mask throwing your wife to the ground.

What action do you take?

He knocks you to the ground and calls you a wussy Momma's boy and invites you to just sit there and watch because you might learn something.

What action do you take now? There is no time to call for help. Do you sit there and let her scream as the masked man rips at her clothing?

What if you have to make him bleed?

What if you have to kill him?

Is God okay with that?

If your answers to these last questions match what you have learned from the Book of Mormon, it is not only our deep animal instinct to protect our women with ferocity, but it is our God-given responsibility to do so. He made us as men naturally protective and ferocious—the perfect guardians for His precious daughters.

Would it matter if the man is bigger than you? No. If you think back now to the way your body felt while I was telling the story. Imagine even more how your body would feel if you had to go through this experience in real life. You would feel a powerful combination of fear, anger, panic and love. These feelings are the result of a chemical spill in your mind that we call "Warrior Chemistry" (in women we call it Mother-Bear Chemistry).

I am convinced that God instilled in our bodies this set of chemical shifts designed specifically to be used in times of battle to actually make us stronger, quicker and more protective when our women and children are under attack. These chemical shifts allow normally small, weak men and women to be able to overcome an enemy far stronger or faster.

I have observed that these chemicals not only empower our bodies to be more powerful and effective in fighting the enemies of our loved ones, it also empowers the body to fight biochemical warfare with Satan. These chemicals neutralize the debilitating chemicals used by Satan. In layman's terms, a warrior can tell when he has successfully changed his body chemistry when "like dragons" (Mosiah 20:11) he does fight.

In our culture, these warrior chemicals and their related feelings are rarely accessed, primarily because they are rarely needed. In most modern cultures, men do not usually have to physically fight invading Lamanites as the Nephites did. Unfortunately, it leaves our men untrained in using Warrior Chemistry and in protecting their families. In the Sons of Helaman program, young men are trained to use this biochemical weapon quickly and instinctively. They learn to use techniques found in the military, sports and music. As with the men of the Book of Mormon, our young warriors combine these temporal skills with their spiritual training, so they can kill Lamanites on Saturday and still be able to teach Priesthood on Sunday.

Practical Application

Before a warrior can use this weapon correctly, he must be trained to recognize when his chemicals are being manipulated by Satan. This means, instead of setting the alarm at the normal masculine awareness, (deviant thoughts—level 3); the alarm is moved up the scale as close to zero as possible. When the alarm is at level three, by the time an individual recognizes that their thoughts are deviant, it's probably too late. The body is so full of the deviant chemicals that most of the will to win is already lost. The signal the deviant chemicals send to the brain causes the energy of the brain to leave the frontal lobe (the values system) and move to the mid-brain (the animal).

In treatment, by moving the alarm up to levels one (chemical) or two (feelings), the individual is alerted to chemical spills at the very earliest levels, prior to reaching the point of no return. This increased discernment is one of the crucial skills taught in the Sons of Helaman program (details later). The warrior must learn to feel very subtle shifts in his brain chemistry and feelings. When he does, his alarm goes off.

When the alarm goes off, the individual initiates a process of intentionally changing his own body chemistry and activating his "warrior chemistry." An increase in the Spirit of Discernment is required to acquire this increased sensitivity. Similar to the way a wine tester increases his sensitivity toward the subtle differences with practice, we set up situations in the group setting designed to increase discernment of shifting feelings and body chemistry within the young man.

Along with increased awareness, we work to increase intensity and speed of response. To facilitate this, we work to make use of the same part of the brain that is used by military men in battle situations when they are asleep. As a military man falls asleep in a battle situation, he sharpens his "listening" skills for any sound that could represent danger. He puts his "adrenaline bucket" nearby so that as soon as he hears the snap of a twig, he will be flooded with the energy necessary to fight quickly. With increased sensitivity, the warrior fighting against addiction will be able to feel slight chemical shifts (snap of a twig). With practice, he can flood his body with warrior chemistry within seconds.

Warrior chemistry is a combination of anger, love, determination, and ferocity. This is the same response the men of the Book of Mormon used to protect their lives, wives and children: "Like dragons did they fight" (Mosiah 20:11). In that chapter, you may remember, the Nephites of King Limhi were outnumbered 2-1 by a ferocious Lamanite army who "fought like lions for their prey." By fighting "for their lives, for their wives and for their children" these outnumbered soldiers were able to decimate a hopelessly larger enemy.

Satan is just as intent on enslaving valiant young men today as the Lamanites were intent on enslaving the people of Limhi. He is fighting "like a lion", and will not stop fighting as long as there is a chance of success. Satan unleashes all his forces to put us in bondage. Most addicts feel like they are fighting a battle outnumbered at least 2-1, if not infinitely more. However, just as the Nephite soldiers used warrior chemistry to win a hopeless battle, I have seen many young men overcome addictions in the exact same way. Today, the battle against addictions is just as real as the Nephites' battles against the Lamanites. The Lamanites would destroy families through slavery, and Satan would destroy families through addictions. This is not a battlefield for halfhearted soldiers. In my experience, a man, young or old, not yet experiencing these chemicals associated with intense ferocity, is not yet fighting hard enough.

How Ferocious do I Really Need to Get?

It is mature and appropriate, when we are under attack by a foe, to first attempt to resolve the problem with dignified diplomacy. If someone enters your space and shows signs of wanting to intrude upon your rights (e.g., kill you, assault your wife and take your children for slaves), you may first try to talk them out of it in a firm, but controlled tone of voice.

If this does not work to dissuade him, unfortunately, you may have to turn to a less dignified form of "communication" in order to successfully protect yourself and your loved ones. These more intense interventions can be uncomfortable.

I am convinced that one of the amazing strategies Satan has been using during this time in history is to keep men from feeling the need to experience the higher levels of ferocity needed to truly protect one's family. This leaves men unprepared when he attacks. Throughout much of recorded history, it has not been uncommon for men to carry weapons with them at all times, because there may have been threats of a significant nature to them and their families at all times.

When we are taught that Satan wants to destroy families, we need to take it seriously. His reputation, "the Serpent was the most subtle of all the beasts of the field," remains true. His attacks on the human mind really are intended to destroy families. He really does work on the minds of men until they are distorted enough to hurt their own wives. And worse, he is so cunningly convincing that some men think they are justified in doing so. They will verbally, physically, or sexually abuse their wives and feel completely justified in doing so after experiencing addictive behaviors for a time. Satan really does want to assault our women, and successfully does so through the unkindness of the husbands, through inappropriate sexuality, etc. This vicious attack also affects the children, who are often tempted and stolen away while the parents are incapacitated.

As we discussed in the Satanic Spin, after a great deal of research and observation, I have discovered that the chemistry of the brain has a great deal to do with the decision making process. With careful and meticulous efforts using carefully crafted thoughts, Satan can trigger chemical changes in the brain that cause a man to lose touch with his values system and make decisions that are damaging to himself and others. The "antidote" to this mind distorting set of chemical shifts is released into the brain of a man when he feels the same feelings he would feel if he needed to protect his family from violence. This level of ferocity often elicits thoughts and words that are not common in the man's language. If I were put in a situation where I either had to kill a 20 year old soldier from another country or let him kill my wife and children, I would experience some strong feelings about it. If he were bigger than me, I would need these strong feelings and the chemicals associated with them in order to have sufficient strength to protect my loved ones. The chemical shifts associated with these feelings are just as effective in strengthening the brain and empowering it to override the subtle, debilitating chemicals triggered by satanic efforts.

For the untrained out there, if you are going to beat this, you are going to have to do the little things with great ferocity! When it is time to read, FIGHT to read! When it is time to pray, FIGHT to pray! When it is time to empty the dishwasher, FIGHT to empty it. When it is time to do homework, FIGHT to get it done! When it is time to NOT turn on the TV, start the computer or play a video game, FIGHT!

Warrior Chemistry in Action

I asked a client how Warrior Chemistry had helped him in his battles, and he wrote back the following:

"There are many ways to fight the adversary; many sing hymns, quote scripture, or try to think of spiritual things. I've tried all those things many times and quite honestly it hardly worked for me. I had to combine something temporal along with my spiritual tactics. I had a very hard time fighting off the devil on my own. I didn't have the proper tools, until I started the Sons of Helaman program. There I learned more tools to fight against Satan. Not only was I shown how to use them, but how to use them effectively.

"The one tool I use today and will use forever is...'warrior chemistry', also known as protective anger.

"In order to learn how to use this tool I had to learn how to imagine myself in different situations, such as fighting off someone trying to take advantage of one of my friends or mom. Science has demonstrated that your mind doesn't know the difference between imagined experiences and the real thing. You will feel the same feelings imagining it as if it is actually happening. To be effective with this tool I had to learn how to do drills, so at a moment's notice when I needed it, the warrior chemical release would become automatic. To do this I allowed myself to feel a little drip of the deviant sex chemical then used my warrior chemistry to get rid of the feeling. I've done it so

many times now that it has become automatic, I can't tell you how much it has changed my life. I finally feel free and I finally feel like I have some control over my life." –C.F.

Call to Arms

A young man is walking through his day doing good things, and Satan observes that if he stays on this path, he is going to become a significant contributor in the fight for good. Satan starts by flashing ideas in the young man's mind, almost instantly causing subtle chemical reactions. The trained warrior realizes almost instantly that he is being messed with, and he is not okay with that. He detects that his chemical state is being altered and immediately activates his "warrior chemistry" feeling protective anger against his enemy who would destroy him and his family. The deviant chemicals are neutralized and the warrior's chemicals, feelings and thoughts return to normal. Values, creative problem solving and determination all come back. To finish off the enemy in this battle, the young man follows through on his training to do something good in that moment of crisis, above and beyond what he would typically do. If the chosen activity makes the life of a woman more comfortable, this is even better.

Because one of Satan's main goals with sexual addiction is to hurt women, inflicting pain and making them cry, anytime these warriors bring a smile to a woman's face, they have defeated the enemy! Yes, he will be back, but the warrior can continue to punish him for attacking.

The Need to be on a Team

When a person of any age falls into addiction, it usually takes more help and training than can be accessed alone. They must understand that the need for help is nothing to be ashamed of. It is not a sign of courage or strength to offer to run into the jungles of Vietnam by yourself in an attempt to win a battle. The humility of knowing when it is time to align yourself with a team often is life or death.

If you struggle to fight more demons than you can handle alone, it means that Satan is so intimidated by you that he has assigned a lot of demons to attack you. This mean you are a bigger threat than you thought! Get help! Get the training you need! Align yourself with a team. You have too many God ordained works to accomplish in your life to just sit around miserably bound by these chains.

Those who battle addiction must do all they can to overcome on their own. Self-sufficiency builds self-confidence. You will have many successes! When the enemy starts to cheat and hits you with more than you can handle, it is an indication that you are a bigger threat than you thought. The proper training will help ensure your success. You have too many God- ordained works to accomplish in your life. It is time to be on a team.

Chapter 7

The Counter-Attack

Just like Moroni's soldiers from our story, today there are many of God's faithful soldiers drinking Satan's contaminated water. The Adversary knows how potentially dangerous these young warriors can be to his kingdom and he won't take any chances. He uses his keen intellect and 7,000 years of manipulating experience to debilitate bright and promising warriors.

I decided that I couldn't sit back and let Satan get away with this spiritual sabotage. I had to do something. The young men that Satan was doping up and dragging into addiction needed to learn how to fight back. They needed to learn about warrior chemistry and other tools that enhance their spiritual fight against the adversary. So in response to his efforts to destroy the lives of our young men, I have worked closely with God and other dedicated professional to bring together the...

Sons of Helaman™

The Sons of Helaman is a group of young men who have dedicated themselves to helping each other overcome unwanted addictive behaviors, primarily those of a sexual nature. In a "Knights of the Round Table" environment, they encourage and help their brethren in the fight against this demon that assails them. With the guidance of a Master's

Degree level clinician, they practice and develop the warrior instincts that are required to conquer these addictions for the rest of their lives. They learn the strategies that the adversary will use against them and are trained how to use the most powerful weapons to defeat him.

Graduation from the program requires successfully conquering the addiction for 12 consecutive weeks. By this time the young man has acquired a healthy fear of the power of Satan and a reverent alliance with the power of God. He will have practiced calling upon the power of God to serve himself as well as those he has grown to love. He will have gained a familiarity with the words of the prophets and will discover how they apply to real life. He will have gained an unusual amount of control over his thoughts, feelings, and body chemistry that will serve him throughout his lifetime. After graduation, the young men are encouraged to return as often as they wish, free of charge (as long as they keep winning), for the brotherhood and continued education.

The young men who are experiencing this training find it to be much more enjoyable and much more effective than individual therapy. Each group is facilitated by a licensed mental health clinician who has been personally certified by the Director, Maurice W. Harker, CMHC. Parents and bishops have been pleased with the cost efficiency being approximately one-fourth the cost of individual therapy. When a group has more than eight members, another group is formed. As one individual graduates, a new member is added.

In this next section I will outline how the group therapy works. I will teach you many of the principles for addiction recovery. As you read and apply them you will be given tools to fight and win against the demon that assails you. You will be able to come off conqueror and live a life pure and worthy, happy and free. Fight as much as you can on your own, but if you are unable to achieve sufficient success, join a team!

Part III

The Battle Plan

Chapter 8

The Team Process

There is great power in fighting against the enemy in teams - not unlike a military troop. I will describe in this chapter how the team/group process works in Sons of Helaman. You will be empowered to conquer the addictions faster if you understand the following. You are welcome to do your best to implement this process on your own. Training is available for those who wish to create Prevention training teams of their own.

Group sessions work best when there are more than three and fewer than nine participants. The team meets once a week for just less than two hours. If interest in the group exceeds eight members, an additional group will be started once four or five more individuals show interest. Each group is intended to be on–going. When one member graduates a new member can take his place. This allows for participation from individuals at every level of progress. More advanced young men can mentor the beginners. Beginners eventually become leaders.

Before joining a team, there is a one hour visit with the young man and his parents (if he is a minor) with the group facilitator. In this meeting we make sure the program is a good fit for the young man and teach him and his parents the basic principles behind the work we do.

When a new group member comes to his first meeting, everyone introduces himself using only first names (for confidentiality reasons) and sharing something interesting about himself.

Each warrior is expected to record days of success (no misbehaviors) and days that contained lost battles with different markings on a calendar. This has proven to be a very relevant part of their training. This calendar is used to track points and progress. Also, after reading this book, each young man is encouraged to purchase the book, *Putting on the Armor of God,* by Steven A. Cramer. Important basic concepts about fighting these addictions can be learned from this book. We commonly refer to it as "The Green Book". This book is not intended to be read quickly, but steadily until completing the book. Parents are also encouraged to read the book and discuss what they learn with the young man (and the whole family if inspired to do so).

Team Motivation

As a form of positive pressure, a reward is provided when the group point average is high enough. At the beginning of the team meeting, the facilitating clinician asks each young man to report his points for the week. The points are totaled and averaged. If the average of the points per young man is equal to or greater than 1.5, pizza will be ordered for the group. Time is allowed (half hour) for the maximum number of young men to show before the "pizza call" is made. Points of first timers are not counted. Pizza seems to be a universal motivator. We find that the young men are highly motivated to contribute, and not detract from the group average. Surprisingly, the young men are very honest about their points. In this kind of group the others can usually tell if one tries to lie.

Calculating Progress Points

Each week at the beginning of the group session the young men will report their points. Points are calculated as follows: On a calendar, the young man is to record each day whether or not he succeeded that day (no pornography or masturbation) or lost at least one battle. On the day of the group meeting he will total the number of successful days in the last 7 days, and he will compare that to the total number of successful days in the week before. For every day that he does better this week compared to the last week he gets 1 point. If he does worse, than he gets -1 point for each day he does worse.

Example: If during the most recent week he had 4 successful days and during the previous week he had 3 successful days: He improved one day so he reports 1 point. If he had 4 successful days during the most recent week and 5 successful days the previous week, he reports -1pts.

If the youth has two perfect weeks back to back, he reports 2 points and informs the group what week (consecutive) he has achieved.

Individuals who complete 4 consecutive perfect weeks achieve the rank of Lieutenant, those who reach 8 weeks, the rank of Captain, and at 12 weeks, the rank of General. Each of these achievements is awarded and celebrated as we will describe in the following chapter.

After points and weeks are calculated, the group member who has the most consecutive weeks of success has first option of running the group. One must be at least a Lieutenant in order to run the group. He begins the discussion by asking each member of the group to respond to the questions from the Captain's Log (which we will discuss in the next chapter). Each warrior answers question #1 before moving on to question #2. The Lieutenant is expected to follow inspiration during the process. The therapist interjects and educates along the way as needed. The questions should be asked in order. They have been carefully created over many years of research and experience. During this time the group facilitating clinician and the lead warrior work hard together to keep the room spiritually strong and warrior intense. Extra time is given to individual young men as needed. It is often the case that all can learn from the needs of the individual.

In the last half hour, emphasis will be given to a discussion on patterns of lost battles (question #5). Individuals who have not figured out how to defeat the enemy in a specific attack will discuss the patterns used against them. Ideas will be exchanged, looking for ways to win in the future.

In the final ten minutes, the young men will participate in the Brotherhood Ritual. This includes standing in a circle and each young man proceeds from brother to brother in the circle shaking his hand, looking him in the eyes and repeats:

***"I promise that I will be of service to you,
and I will allow you to be of service to me,
until both you and I successfully defeat
this demon that assails us."***

The receiving brother responds with, "Thank You". The young men take this commitment to each other very seriously.

Progress in Group

Getting Started. Often, gaining momentum is the hardest part. Each warrior understands that at any time along the way, if he has a single "lost battle" he must return to zero weeks and start over. This pressure ensures that the brain will prepare itself to win battles for the rest of the man's life!

4 Weeks—Lieutenant. When an individual has achieved 4 consecutive weeks of success, he then becomes a Lieutenant. At this time he is awarded the Lieutenant's wristband. This is often the most difficult phase. The young men have a strong drive to be a leader in the group and so they make a special effort to succeed. The Lieutenant is now qualified to lead the group discussion (along with the supervising clinician). The Lieutenant has the responsibility to learn to be inspired in this process.

6 Weeks—Fighting S.P. & S.S. The bar is raised at 6 weeks when the battle shifts its focus to the more subtle elements including Soft Porn (little brother to pornography) and Self-Stimulation (little brother to masturbation). After 6 weeks, if the warrior visits with SP or SS, he drops back to 6 weeks (instead of going all the way back to 0 weeks). Points are calculated the same: visits with SP and/or SS are considered 2nd level lost battles.

8 Weeks—Captain. When an individual has achieved 8 consecutive weeks, he becomes a Captain. He is rewarded with a medallion that represents Sons of Helaman principles. He is responsible to continue sharing with his brethren the keys to success during the final stage. Between 8 and 12 weeks he is also required to achieve 28 "perfect MAN PoWeR" days. The details of this are discussed in the MAN PoWeR journal.

12 Weeks—General. When a young man reaches this level, he graduates from the program and becomes a General. He has gained the skills necessary to beat this enemy for a lifetime. A ritualistic award ceremony takes place. The young man receives the coveted "SONS OF HELAMAN" ring to be worn for his lifetime to remind him of his success and the necessity to stay ever vigilant. The young man is asked to use the skills he has gained by serving his brethren who are still struggling. This effort will help him crystallize his acquired skills and transition into the next phase of his life, which hopefully includes serving a mission and/or temple marriage. He is invited to return to the group as often as he wishes for free, as long as he keeps winning.

Text Coaching™

I can't tell you how many times I have had a mother contact me in powerless desperation because they have a dearly loved son that needs help, but is too embarrassed, or afraid, or proud to ask for it. Not only mothers, but fathers and wives and bishops have approached me with the same dilemma. In the past, I tried several different ways to help these individuals, but they have always been insufficient. Too many of our loved ones who have not been able to live up to their own expectations are falling through the cracks.

Also, there are graduates who need help avoiding relapse, as well as warriors in Sons of Helaman who just need an extra push. I have pondered for years how to help these young men—and I have finally found a solution. And as usual, "...by small and simple things are great things brought to pass" (Alma 37:6). I have found a simple weapon that if used properly is extremely useful for the long-distance addict, the warrior avoiding relapse, and all other addicts as well. This weapon is Text Coaching.

Text Coaching is so simple and powerful. I am almost embarrassed that it took me this long to find a way to make it work. As you know, it is not uncommon to find that individuals with addictions and compulsive behaviors can succeed for a period of time, but then they lose momentum and "**fall off the wagon**". Text-Coaching (or T-Coaching, as it is often called) takes advantage of modern social media technology (texting) and allows struggling warriors to automatically receive several therapeutically formulated text messages each day from a Certified Text Coach. In these texts the client is asked carefully crafted questions designed to **train their brains** to overcome addictive and/or compulsive behaviors. For maximum benefit, the client is encouraged to answer every text. These **answers go directly to** their personally assigned Text Coach, who assesses the answers to see if the state of mind of the client is strong enough for them to "win their battles" until they get their next text. The Text Coach will provide **short interventions** via text about once per day. By winning for shorter periods of time the client gains the momentum needed to help them succeed for a life time.

Why is Text Coaching So Effective?

Text Coaching is effective because it allows thumb-tip access to professional help. When an addict first feels under attack, they are only one text away from instant support and motivation.

Text Coaching is effective because it increases the frequency of coaching. Many who fight addictions and compulsive behaviors can't last a full week. Daily intervention through text coaching can make the difference between falling off the band wagon or not; and it is far more affordable than weekly treatment.

Text Coaching is effective because it costs less. Text coaching is less than half the price of even a low-end weekly group therapy session, where the addict will be seen only once a week.

Text coaching is effective because the client retains anonymity. Many struggling warriors resist seeking help due to humiliation. They want help, but they are afraid of exposing themselves as addicts. Text Coaching allows anonymity from other clients. This can also prove a good first step towards more intense treatment, if desired.

Text Coaching At Work

One warrior, after using the Text Coaching program, wrote the following:

"At first, I wasn't enthusiastic about using Text Coaching. I was already attending group therapy sessions and I didn't want to spend the extra $20 a week just for someone to text me. I didn't need that—or so I thought.

"Somehow, I don't remember exactly how, I got signed up, and I am eternally grateful I did—it has become a key to my success. Despite my initial hesitancy, I soon came to look at each text as a challenge—a challenge to see if I was man enough to answer. I made a game out of it. I wouldn't receive a single text without answering it, even when sometimes the texts came at busy times.

"The hardest part was when I had to confess I had not been keeping my goals like marking my calendar, or running my border patrol. 'Dang it!' I would think when the text came, 'I have to do that again!' Looking back, that discomfort was exactly what I needed. I needed to be consistently reminded of the daily actions I needed to take, especially when I had been slacking.

"I have been a graduate of the Sons of Helaman for over 6 months and I continue to use Text Coaching. I have noticed a significant difference in my battles depending on my faithfulness in responding to my texts. When I have been lax in responding, thinking, 'I have this under control', those have been the moments when I have been hardest hit. I love Text Coaching because it helps me stay focused all day long every day.

`"I hope many more young men will apply this program seriously. I am convinced that it is a powerful tool for overcoming the enemy that assails us."

--Jim

Consistency Matters

"It doesn't work!" some warriors exclaim after receiving the daily texts and experiencing no improvement in their ability to fight battles. "It's just a waste of time and money. I signed up, but nothing changed."

When they say this, I ask them a few questions. "How many of the texts have you responded to?"

"Um...well...I have responded to some of them."

"Okay, how often have you responded would you say—on average? Once a day? Twice a week? Once a week?"

If they're honest they usually answer, "Once a day, maybe every other day. It depends."

When I hear this I begin teaching my "IT" principle. When someone calls into IT technical support for help with a computer that isn't working, before asking any complicated questions, the IT representative will ask: "Is your computer plugged in? Did you try hitting the power button?" This may be a no brainer, but often times the client will say, "Oh, wait, it wasn't plugged in," or "where is the power button?" For a computer to work it has to be turned on, for Text Coaching to work, you have to "turn it on" by responding. Just signing up will not magically remove the addict's habits, but it does give the warrior an ideal opportunity to daily remind himself why he is fighting and how he must do it.

I cannot stress enough the importance of actually replying to the text messages. Even if the answers are one sentence answers, or even one-word answers. Just the act of responding consistently puts the warrior's brain in a different mindset.

Text coaching works. It works when it is used. Like any tool, if it is left on the shelf it is useless. Simply receiving text messages is not going to change much, but consistently responding to 6 text messages a day—that will make a difference.

If you are receiving Text Coaching and are not satisfied with the results you are receiving, I have a challenge for you. In the next two weeks, respond to *every* Text Coaching text as soon as you can, even if it is one word. Be completely honest, if you haven't run to your Flag Pole, or written on your calendar, say so—and then go do it.

Do this for two weeks and then use your internal scanning skills to see what changes have happened to you over the previous two weeks. It is a cool experience. Try it out.

Captain's Log

A military Captain will often write down his thoughts for future reference, or just to clarify what is going on in his mind. A successful warrior will ask and answer the following questions frequently in a personal journal or notebook. In the following chapter, we will take an in depth look at these powerful questions.

1) "Why are you fighting?" "Why don't you just give up?"

2) "How did you win your most difficult recent battle?" "What have you been doing right when you win?"

3) "What are you doing to help pay for your work in this program?" "Are you keeping a daily calendar?" "Do you think about these things when temptation is knocking at the door?"

4) "What are you doing for Border Patrol activities?" "Do you have meaningful rituals in place?" "Are they sufficient?" "What is your Flag Pole/Passion Project?" "How is your Border Patrol system different from those with more than 8 weeks?"

5) "When you lost, what technique did the enemy use to defeat you?" "Is there a pattern?" "If you could replay the event, what could you have done to beat him?" "What drills can you do to make sure you win next time if he tries something similar?"

6) "What might the enemy try in the future?" "What do you need to do to be prepared for such an attack?"

Chapter 9

The Training

Now I am going to walk you through the steps of what goes on in the treatment and training side of the Sons of Helaman program. You are welcome to do your best with this training on your own or with your loved ones. A concerted effort will help many improve significantly. Below you will find the 6 sets of questions from the Captain's Log that are reviewed in every group session. These questions have been carefully formulated over many years of research, experience and inspiration.

Question #1: Why are you fighting? Why don't you just give up?

This is the most important question, and we spend the most time on it. It is interesting to watch the reaction of each young man when I ask these questions, especially the new guys. I can often tell how bad the addiction is by how long it takes him to answer the two questions and how much depth there is to the answers. In order to answer these questions, the individual must move into the values part of his brain (Frontal Lobe). As mentioned earlier, in order for a good man to do bad things, he must lose connection with his value system and drift into his animal brain, where values are not relevant. The time it takes him to travel back to his values system tells me how far away from his value system he is.

Unfortunately, it is the nature of all things on this earth to deteriorate. Buildings fall apart, the ground grows weeds, bodies lose their shape, and brains (especially male brains) drift away from things that matter. In order for a human brain to stay strong, it must be exercised.

As if dealing with atrophy is not enough, then you add the factor of a strong, negative entity (Satan) who is personally interested in the destruction of your buildings, and casting the seeds of tares (weeds) into your soil. Now, not only do you have to do the work it takes to maintain your buildings, land, body and mind, but you also must fight to protect them.

Going through the process of answering the questions that go with #1 strengthens the individual's "body", maintains their "buildings", weeds their "gardens", and returns the mind to the values system. With respect to protecting the mind, training techniques used in military training, athletic training and music training are used. Drills, drills, and more drills.

It is important to remind the reader that an individual's true self is found in the values system. It is my belief that this is where one's Spirit resides. When there are so many "voices" running around in one's mind, it is hard to know who you really are. I tell my clients, "You know who you are by what you *plan* to do." Conscious plans are formulated in the values system part of the brain. As the time comes to execute those plans, as they say, all hell breaks loose in an effort to knock you off track. Satan uses whatever he can, both inside and outside of you, to keep your plans from coming to fruition.

The Creepy Guy Detector™

One reason many young men fight is for women: the young women around them and their future wife. No young man wants to have to confess to his girlfriend or fiancé that he is struggling with a sexual addiction. Men naturally want to impress the women they love and be looked up to as a hero. Sexual misbehavior is neither impressive nor heroic and young men know that. Virtuous young women are often a powerful motivator for young men.

Women also have a special gift of intuition enabling them to recognize that something is "not quite right" with the men around them. We call this the Creepy Guy Detector.

One warrior from the Sons of Helaman had the following experience with the Creepy Guy Detector.

"I was on a date a little over a week ago, and the subject came around to Pornography. Now for the unprepared guy, I guess, that would be an awkward conversation, to say the least. But for me, I am ready, and I expect it. I hope my sister and all other young women have the courage to ask the necessary questions. I hope young men have the guts to give young women honest answers!

"My friend felt seriously scarred by pornography. Two men she had dated, one of which she had almost married, had been porn addicts, which led to them treating her like an object. 'I've learned so much since then,' she said. 'I knew all along that there was something wrong, but I just didn't know what it was.'

"When a wife or a mother to a porn addict discovers the problem, almost everyone says the same thing, 'I knew something was wrong, but I didn't know what.' Women seem to have a sixth sense that tells them, 'Whoa! Wait a minute! Something is not right here.' The name we give to this power is the 'Creepy Guy Detector'. Girls who learn to recognize and validate this sensation can often discern a porn addict just by 'sensing' him.

"I hadn't yet told my friend about this when she said, 'You'll think I'm weird, but I can just tell now when a guy has a problem or not. Usually just by looking into his eyes, but for sure when I hug him. By the time I've finished hugging him I can tell whether he is a porn addict or not.'

"I'm really good at it. With every guy who has set off my senses and I have confronted, he has admitted he has a problem. Not a single guy I've been wrong about. I'm just totally honest with them, 'do you look at pornography?' and they tell me. Sometimes they break out and start crying.

"The Creepy Guy Detector, I believe is a gift from God, for women to be able to protect themselves. Heavenly Father 'delights in the chastity of women' (Jacob 2:28). He loves to see them happy and clean and free. He knows the pain that untrained sexual addicts will bring them, and has blessed them with this extra sense."

Those currently misbehaving at an addict level need to be aware of this. If you think you're hiding this and no one knows, you're only fooling yourself. The women in your life know. They may not know exactly what is wrong, but they know something is wrong. When a wife or mother finds out about a sexual problem their husband or son has had, the almost universal response is, "I knew something was wrong, I didn't know what, but now I do."

Many addicts use the Creepy Guy Detector as motivation to keep fighting. "Why are you fighting?" "So I can date girls and their Creepy Guy Detector won't go off." Becoming free of addiction, not only frees yourself, but it also frees up emotionally all the women who love you and care about you.

Question #2: "How did you win your most difficult recent battle?" "What have you been doing right when you win?"

With this question, each young man reviews his methods of success. I will describe some of the ideas and activities we hope they learn to apply.

One of the most powerful drills I have seen warriors use is to build the habit of daily journaling at least 3 answers to the questions, "Why are you fighting? Why don't you give up?" The warrior will be tempted to just think about the answers instead of writing them down. This is like a basketball player who thinks about free-throws versus a player who actually practices the free-throws. Mental practice has its value, but it will never be as good as practicing the real action over and over again.

Write down three reasons per day! Minimum! Some make a ritual of writing them down first thing in the morning, others write them before they go to bed. Some write this Captain's Log in their MAN PWR Journal. Some text or email these answers to supporting friends and family. Those Sons of Helaman enrolled in Text Coaching are asked all six questions daily via texts from Certified Text Coaches. Warriors must find a method that works for them that prompts them to remind themselves why they are fighting, and what it will take to win. In group sessions, warriors work together to make sure everyone gives answers strong enough to overcome the enemy.

The answers usually change over time. Reasons for fighting for beginners are usually idealistic yet create no increase in energy or release of warrior chemistry. We call these "canned answers". This is because the answers are as if the young man just opened up a can on a shelf and gave his answer. It is the answer he is "supposed" to give, but there is very little feeling behind it. The veterans who have experience will attempt to teach the new young man that he is going to have to sharpen his reasons if they are going to work. For beginners, they often have to tap into more base reasons, like, "I hate how I feel right afterwards." "I want to get control back in my life." "I am losing important things/events in my life."

The Book of Mormon teaches us many important things about how to successfully fight in a battle. It discusses the importance of using both Spiritual and Temporal (of the body) powers. Before going into a battle, the warrior must make sure his connection to God is solid. The warrior must remember his dependence on God. He must recommit his loyalty. Then, as the enemy crosses lines toward your loved ones, a transition takes place. As one of our prophets in modern times has said, "Pray as if it all depends on God; act as if it all depends on you."

The righteous warriors of the Book of Mormon demonstrated the need for ferocity in times of battle. "...they fought for their lives, and for their wives, and for their children; therefore they exerted themselves and ***like dragons*** did they fight" (Mosiah 20:11, emphasis added). The warrior must find reasons that stoke this ferocity, otherwise known as "releasing warrior chemistry". This has been mentioned in previous chapters. Because Satan is not using actual swords and cimeters in this modern form of warfare, but body chemistry instead, our warriors must use body chemistry as a weapon to fight back.

When listing reasons for fighting, the warrior needs to keep digging in to his heart and mind until he finds a reason that triggers the release of warrior chemistry into his body. This is most easily done with men who have daughters. All I have to do is help them imagine some stranger attempting to do unfortunate things to their daughters, and the warrior chemistry floods in.

Married men do well if they imagine their wives are under attack. With young men it is more challenging. Most of our young men have never needed to tap into that degree of ferocity. Those that have a history of serious sports involvements have at least experienced the beginnings of warrior chemistry.

Sometimes I have to connect the dots to help the young men see how these invitations to misbehave are intended to make them feel stupid, but more so, to make their future wives cry. Almost universally, the married men that I work with were addicts while teenagers. They had every intention of stopping the misbehaviors before and during their marriages, but they have been unable to do so. Now their biggest nightmare has arrived. "Ye have broken the hearts of your tender wives, and lost the confidence of your children, because of your bad examples before them; and the sobbings of their hearts ascend up to God against you" (Jacob 2:35).

If you are reading this book for your own welfare, please, every day write down the reasons you are fighting against this addiction until you feel the warrior chemistry raging through your blood! One reason I have found text coaching to be so effective is that the warrior has to type out every day *why* he is fighting. Whether you are enrolled in text coaching or not, physically writing down your motivation will make a difference.

I was once asked the following question, "What role does the enabling power of Jesus Christ play in what you teach?"

Throughout scriptural history, there has been a fascinating balance between the efforts of men and the power of God, especially in military type situations. We find stories like David vs. Goliath, Moses vs. Pharaoh, Ammon vs. the evil band of Lamanites, The Sons of Helaman vs. the Lamanites, Gideon and his men vs. the Midianites, etc., etc. In each case, we observe a seemingly small force against a much larger force. In each case we find the smaller force tightly tied into the power of God. In each case the smaller force fights with full ferocity.

Mosiah 20:11: "And it came to pass that the people of Limhi began to drive the Lamanites before them; yet they were not half so numerous as the Lamanites. But they fought for their lives, and for their wives, and for their children; therefore they exerted themselves and **like dragons** did they fight" (emphasis added).

This is all well and good, but it does not clarify what role God and his power play in the fight. Other stories describe it more thoroughly. When David confronts Goliath, he uses a very accurate combination of warrior chemistry and an understanding of the vital role of the power of God.

1 Samuel 17:45: "Then said David to the Philistine, Thou comest to me with a sword, and with a spear, and with a shield: but I come to thee in the name of the Lord of hosts, the God of the armies of Israel, whom thou hast defied.

46 "This day will *the Lord deliver thee* into mine hand; and **I will smite thee, and take thine head from thee**; and I will give the carcasses of the host of the Philistines this day unto the fowls of the air, and to the wild beasts of the earth; that all the earth may know that there is a God in Israel" (emphasis added).

David has a clear understanding (at the age of a youth!) of the need for a combination of the power of God and his own intense efforts. We hope the young men will learn a similar balance.

Question #3: "What are you doing to help pay for your work in this program?" "Are you keeping a daily calendar?" "Do you think about these things when temptation is knocking at the door?"

Wallet Motivation

It has been observed that when an individual has a financial investment in something, he puts more effort into its success. The same is true of Sons of Helaman. If he cannot afford to pay for his own visits, he is strongly encouraged to do service in exchange for whoever is making his payments. Many clients, when asked question #1, "Why are you fighting?" answer, "I'm fighting so I don't have to pay Maurice anymore." One client, we'll call him Tom, figured out how much money it cost him every time he lost a battle and had to start over from week 0. Tom would remember that amount every time he was tempted to give in and ask himself, "Would this experience really be worth it?" This mentality helped him overcome his addiction.

Calendar

A calendar should be marked every day showing whether or not it was a "perfect day" (no lost battles). This is used to build healthy pressure in the mind as he works toward 12 perfect weeks, and helps us discover patterns.

Often, one of the biggest reasons a new young man will succeed is because of his calendar...he does not want to have "red X's" on his calendar. Also, the threat of ruining pizza for the group is a strong motivator. The discipline to mark the calendar every day is a vital part of the psychological work it takes to beat this addiction.

If a warrior wants to increase the power of his calendar right off the bat, I invite him to put next to each smiley face two things: the number of days consecutive he has won his battles, and the financial consequences of a lost battle at this point. We have calculated that each day in Sons of Helaman to be about $6.42. Add that much to each day and it will show how much it will cost to start over after having a lost battle. Remembering both of these numbers can be a great motivator.

"Where do I put my calendar?" clients will ask me. I tell them to put their calendar in a place where their mother or wife can see it. Why? Because no man wants to put a red-X or a frowny face on a calendar knowing that later that day the woman he loves is going to see it. It is often hard for clients to want to post their lost battles for their mother or wife to see, but it is a powerful motivation. Satan works in dark corners in isolation, God works in light with communication and cooperation. Clients should enlist their spouse or mother to motivate and encourage them and clients should make themselves accountable to these women as well.

The calendar can be very effective. I have seen it work miracles in the lives of some clients. It works especially well during those times when warriors feel overwhelmed. Despite their best efforts, they feel totally incapable of beating Satan all at once (go cold turkey). That is exactly what Satan wants them to feel. When they feel hopeless, they are more likely to give up and give in. Many warriors have been benefited by the mantra, "If you can win for 24 hours, you can win for a life-time."

In my own ferocious determination to fight back, I have found a way, supported by the Holy Ghost and the Atonement of Christ, to turn calendars into an empowering offensive tactile missile to destroy Satan's strategy. I call it the "Line upon Line Battle Strategy." I recommend this primarily for those who have been fighting addiction for several years and are not able to attend Sons of Helaman training meetings.

The Line Upon Line Battle Strategy

We are taught in our religion that our efforts to become perfect can be line upon line, precept upon precept. Even Christ developed grace for grace. The theme behind the battle technique I will be describing here is designed to gradually take back "territory" he has stolen from us.

It is very common for the addict part of the brain to panic when the idea of being neglected for the rest of your life is proposed. In therapy sessions, I observe an involuntary "addict panic" when I propose to one of the warriors an extreme change in behavior that would starve the addict part of the brain forever. The strategy I discuss here is designed to use the "frog in the pot" concept to control the addict part of the brain, instead of it using the same strategy to control the warrior. You will see that this subtle approach keeps the "addict panic" from sabotaging the efforts of the warrior as it has done in the past.

I start by calculating the average number of "good days" the warrior has between "lost battles" over the course of the last 3 months. This does not have to be exact, a rough estimate is sufficient. I then have the warrior pull out a calendar, and from the last lost battle, we mark a :) on that many consecutive days starting from the last lost battle. I then have him put an "x" on the next day.

I then have the warrior remember that he is fully capable of winning, on purpose, for that many days with some determination because he has done so in the past. In almost every case, when the warrior also remembers why he is fighting against the addiction, he can make a commitment to do what it takes to win for that many days with only a hint of fear instead of a flood of fear or panic.

The warrior will still need to use all his weapons (border patrol activities: reading, writing, prayer, warrior chemistry drills, exercise, calendaring, planning, listening, text coaching, etc.) in order to win, but he knows he is fighting toward a land mark, instead of endless and eternal fighting.

The warrior starts by winning all battles on the series of days he has marked with a :). When he gets to the day with an "x" he is allowed to rest. He does not make much of an effort to win. Sometimes he accidentally wins for longer than planned. It is okay either way. He has won for the time he planned. This is a great victory. If and when a lost battle occurs at this point, there will be little pleasure in it, but it will placate the addict part of the brain for now, and the Holy Ghost will only briefly withdraw.

Following the lost battle, the warrior quickly pulls out the calendar and adds one more day of consecutive :)'s than he had last time. If he conquered 4 consecutive days last time, he marks, in advance, 5 days this time on the calendar, followed by a day with an "x" again.

Again, he uses all his skills and weapons to win each day marked with a :). The Holy Ghost is quick to join this battle because the warrior is improving. Perfection is not required to have the Holy Ghost; only determination to become perfect is required.

When the invitation to misbehave surfaces on days marked with a :), the warrior can firmly and easily respond, "It's only one day more than last time, I don't need it yet." Interestingly, like the frog in the pot, the addict part of the brain doesn't fully register the change as much because it is gradual.

As I have seen this strategy in real life practice, after about 5 cycles of this, where the warrior improves just one day in each cycle, the confidence of the warrior starts to skyrocket! Some warriors start to add two or more days instead of just one, although this is not required for the strategy to work.

For those concerned about how ecclesiastical leaders respond to this, it has been my experience that if the improvement is measurable and consistent (without relapse to more frequent lost battles), the leader will validate and reward the warrior for his efforts.

Scientifically speaking, this strategy does amazing things for the brain. Every time the brain experiences winning a mini-battle throughout the days marked with a :), it becomes stronger and the preferred neurological pathways become more likely to be followed in the future. Also, the longer the brain goes without a dose of the addictive deviant chemicals, the less it feels a need for such chemicals. Eventually, the warrior still notices "hits", but they have less of an effect on him. And the strength he has gained from winning all the mini-battles empowers him to win more frequently.

So, how does a warrior begin? Start by estimating the average number of successful days between lost battles over the last few months. Mark that many days out on your calendar to succeed, ":)". And let the war begin! If you are accountable to someone as with text coaching, report each day as "2/4" if you're just finished winning 2 days out of the 4 you are committed to. Or "5/7" if you are on the 5th day of 7.

By the way, you can do the same thing with hours instead of days. Some warriors start losing battles almost every day. Gaining 4 hours can be exciting! Adjust the system to your circumstances as needed.

Question #4: "What are you doing for Border Patrol activities?" "Do you have meaningful rituals in place?" "Are they sufficient?" "What is your Flag Pole/Passion Project?" "How is your Border Patrol system different from those with more than 8 weeks?"

Border Patrol

After the enemy has successfully been removed from a city, a good military organization will set up a border patrol to make sure they know the enemy's next move and are prepared *before* the enemy arrives. When a warrior has begun to seriously fight, it is time to put in place a border patrol system. This is a set of rituals designed to alert the warrior if any danger is lurking. As in a military situation, the border patrol should be done regularly whether there is an imminent threat or not. Once the enemy is kicked out of the city, before it can storm the city again, it must shut down the defenders' border patrol. The warrior who loses his fear of the enemy and stops using his border patrol is practically asking for the enemy to invade, and most likely will be defeated again. We now use the MAN PWR journal to formalize the Border Patrol.

The warrior must find a set of activities that help him to get an answer to the question, "What is the enemy going to try next?" and then become sufficiently prepared for such an attack. The most effective way to do this is to trust God's bird's-eye view of your life more than your own limited view. When a military leader in the Book of Mormon wanted to know where the Lamanites were going to attack next, he asked the prophet and was told what was going to happen in the future so he could prepare for it. A modern day warrior can ask God directly what strategy the enemy is going to try next. The warrior can receive this prophetic revelation, and will be able to prepare for the next attack. This takes practice, but it is a very powerful tool. Young men will be taught this in the group experience.

Successful Border Patrol activities include:

- Reading/listening to the words of the prophets or other inspired works. The goal being to find a new weapon each time. The warrior will need to read/listen until they come across something meaningful (worthy of memorizing).
- Memorizing or reviewing (multiple times per day) powerful quotes (3x5 cards).
- Meaningful prayer – connecting with and consulting with God.
- Intense physical exercise. Stimulating warrior chemistry while exercising.
- Meaningful pondering – thinking about tricks that have been used on you in the past for signs of what might be used in the future.
- Captain's Log or Journal – writing the answers in a notebook.
- Writing Letters to Wife and/or Letters to God journal.

The border patrol should be a consistent routine. These should be a daily part of life, like breathing, eating, or brushing teeth. "My house is a house of order" (D&C 132:18) said the Lord. Satan works in confusion and darkness, God works in light and order. When a warrior has order and structure in his life, it is far more difficult for the enemy to bring him down.

A warrior can tell when he has completed the border patrol process when he feels he can identify with confidence the next Satanic attack strategy and feels prepared for such an attack remaining in "warrior mode" until the next border patrol session.

At 12 weeks, we expect to see the warrior having a complete and effective "border patrol system". Most young warriors who enroll in Sons of Helaman underestimate how much daily "exercise" must be done in order to beat an addiction of this nature. Unfortunately, one must respond with the same degree of intensity as if he were drafted into the military. Many new enrollees hope that the training will not disrupt their normal life routines. As with boot camp, as with the MTC, if the young man does not experience a noticeable change in his daily activities, then there probably has not been a significant change in his *character*. These daily exercises, which we call "border patrol", are designed to keep the young man sharp and well protected.

One of the primary distinguishing factors I look for at the time of graduation in order to predict relapse is, "What is his border patrol system like? Does he follow through without reminders? Does the system he has set up sufficiently re-sharpen his mind every day? Does he recognize and love the value he gains from it?" If you have gotten to 12 weeks and beyond without having set up and sustained your border patrol system, then I am not surprised that you could not maintain your success. It is extremely rare that addictive tendencies will just go away, like hoping Lamanites will stop attacking if you are a Nephite. We expect that they will always attack, some time and somewhere. But if we are alert and well trained, we can win for the rest of our lives.

Scientifically speaking, it takes about 12 weeks for both the neurological structures of the brain and the basic chemical patterns to settle into a new "normal". While it may take about 3 weeks to break or create a habit, breaking addictive behaviors takes longer because the chemical and neurological elements are so much more unignorable. Also, it takes careful training to accurately change the neurological structures of the brain and chemical patterns. If not done correctly, there is no guarantee that the addictive behaviors will be eliminated.

Spiritually speaking, do not forget that there is a malicious and intelligent entity behind all this. Satan knows about your neurological structures. Satan knows about your body chemistry. Satan knows about your potential on this planet. He knows that with momentum, you could discover before you are 19 years old that you actually are very amazing and are fully capable of spending the next 60 years doing miracles on this planet! He is very strategic in his efforts to derail us. In my experience, it takes a minimum of 12 weeks to become familiar with and prepared for all his devious strategies. He is good at what he does, but with proper training, which includes learning how to involve God in the war, we can get to the point where we never have a lost battle again.

For those of you who have reached 12 weeks but feel yourself slipping, I invite you to reinforce your daily border patrol. Use the MAN PWR journal with ferocity. Find a set of activities that keep you sharp, and find someone to be accountable to. Remember, as soon as your guard is down, that is when things get very dangerous. If you would like someone to be accountable to, I highly recommend Text Coaching, which makes you personally accountable for your border patrol, and also allows access to professionals who can help you develop your Border Patrol. Whatever course you take, do it NOW! Running your border patrol is key to keeping your mind protected from enemy invasion.

Running to the Flag Pole

"You know where to go! Get there as quickly and as orderly as you can!" The teacher commands, as the students laugh and giggle. The constant blare of the Fire Alarm seems like it would make the students nervous or afraid, but they aren't. It's just a fire drill, and they know it. At least once a school year they march out of their classrooms to the sound of the sirens. They have run this drill so many times, everyone knows where to go: the flag pole.

Fire drills save lives; when a real fire comes, the students will know exactly what to do and where to go. They don't have to think while the building is burning around them, they just do what they have practiced so many times. This is the principle of the Flag Pole, running an emergency drill over and over again until it becomes second nature.

This principle is key for overcoming addictions as well. When you are in a spiritual burning building, it is an emergency: it is not time to think or plan, it is time to act. In fact, if you wait to make a plan until you're caught in a fire, you will most likely end up losing another battle. The key is to know exactly what to do *before* the fire comes. A skilled warrior drills and drills, so when the "fiery darts of the adversary" come, he is ready.

Every recovering addict or person striving for self-mastery should have a "flag pole" to run to when the danger alarms go off in his head. This should involve an actual physical location where they have to move to get to. For beginners I recommend your mailbox.

One recovering addict ran out to his basketball court in the back yard and had to make a pre-designated number of shots before he went back inside. Another slept in his running clothes with his shoes by the bed. If he was attacked in the middle of the night, without stopping to think or rationalize he would lace up his shoes and race around his block trying to break his fastest record. Another would run out to the stop sign and give it a high five. For another, his flag pole was his mailbox, when tempted, he would go out, stand by his mailbox and just talk.

Sometimes a warrior cannot leave to run to his flag pole. If he is attacked while in a school Biology class, he may not be able to get up and run around the block. A skilled warrior should have a flag pole for these circumstances as well. Activating warrior chemistry and praying can be an effective flag pole to run to. Some warriors look at a picture of Christ, sing a hymn, or recite a scripture in their head. My favorite for those who cannot go anywhere is to have a set of 3x5 cards with power quotes to review over and over again until brain chemistry returns to normal. These power quotes are found/created in moments of inspiration, usually between battles.

As you can see, flag poles can be different for different warriors. In order for a flag pole to be effective, the warrior must have a pre-rehearsed plan which effectively changes his brain chemistry as soon as he feels an attack. He must drill this plan daily, so like the students at school, as soon as temptation comes he will immediately leave the burning building without hesitation or stopping to think, "What should I do now?"

The flag pole must be run daily until it is second nature. Like any athlete, the more successful you want to be, the more you drill. A successful warrior will practice his flag pole daily and run to it as soon as he feels the slightest shift in his brain chemistry. He will also run to it 3 or more times per day just for practice.

An effective flag pole will include the neutralizing drug that Captain Moroni's army in our story would take as soon as they began to feel their water had been polluted. Thinking of their wives and children, the chemicals would shift quickly, without needing to stop and think or rationalize.

Passion Projects

One of the main reasons Satan attacks a warrior is to keep good things from happening. If a warrior becomes very passionate about his contribution to the world, Satan is in trouble. Passion projects make a great Flag Pole to run to in time of attack. Passion projects are good, constructive things you love to do. Take out the drawing pad; go to the piano, or the wood shop. Use some warrior chemistry to clear your head and go out and get something done. Building, creating, working and serving will help redirect your focus and energies into wholesome activities, allowing your brain chemistry to balance out.

Know your passion project(s). Plan to work on them before the attack comes. Practice throwing your whole self into your passion project as soon as temptation knocks on your door. Remember, if you have to think during the fire, you will get burned!

Passion Projects are projects the warrior has a personal interest in and that can take the place of all of the mental, emotional, chemical and physical time and energy that was previously used toward the addiction. This can be almost anything that is meaningful to the warrior. Some warriors have chosen things from the following categories:

- Missionary Preparation
- Exercise/Athletics
- Spiritual Enhancement
- Outdoors activities
- Music skills
- Academics
- Service: Anything that makes someone else's life better!!

One warrior I know wrote a book. Every day, to keep his head clear he would write just a page or two, but it was enough to keep him focused throughout the day. Not only was he able to avoid temptation, but he was able to create something he will be proud of for his whole life. The book is intended to help others.

Passion projects are also vital for long term success against addictions, especially those of a sexual nature. Regular and consistent effort on such projects helps to create a whole new body chemistry system in the mind. Eventually when the warrior feels pain and discomfort, the brain will automatically suggest the passion project instead of "pain relieving" misbehaviors. This long term change in the brain takes time (approximately 1 month for every year the addiction was present – unless Divine assistance accelerates the process).

Bonus: Why drills are so important

The Sons of Helaman program is built around drills. Running to the Flag Pole, Passion Projects, and Border Patrol are all drills that the warrior will run over and over again until they are habit. Why do we do drills? I get asked this question a lot, especially from warriors who are not succeeding and doing drills seems so unimportant and unrelated to the addiction. The answer is to ask any professional—athlete, or musician, or performer—why they practice and do drills. Their answers will be similar: professionals practice *to do things automatically, to become consistent and accurate,* and to *improve the small but critical actions.*

Drills are a set of actions done repeatedly in order to master a certain skill or habit. Pianists play scales, over and over and over again. Basketball players shoot free-throws, shot after shot after shot. Speed and accuracy are key: it's not enough to just be fast, you have to be accurate as well.

In fighting addiction, drills are key as well. Fighting Satan is a lot like being a good basketball player, it takes speed, accuracy and intensity, and each of these skills is gained by drills. How do the drills from the Sons of Helaman build important skills for fighting addiction?

The Flag Pole gives us a pattern to follow when we're under attack. We don't have to think or reason, we just react according to the plan we've practiced over and over and over again. Just as a basketball player in mid-air doesn't have time to *think* through all the steps of a good shot: a good jump, the energy flowing from the knees to the ball, the fingers placed in just the right spot, the shoulders facing the basket squarely and releasing the ball at the perfect time, in just the right way to give it a beautiful backwards spin. So an addict in the time of an attack doesn't have time to think of the elements of fighting Satan: warrior chemistry, get down and do 20 push-ups, run around the block, serve someone, work on a passion project, etc. The crisis isn't the time to prepare. It is the time to execute.

The Border Patrol is a daily drill that ensures that no enemies are invading the warrior's mind or heart, honing his skills to detect an invasion at the first sign of an attack and to be strong enough to repel it.

Good basketball players are made at the free throw line, practicing. Shooting basket after basket, day after day, they improve their technique even *after* it has become second nature. Good spiritual warriors are made on the free throw line of the brain, practicing over and over the Flag Pole and Border Patrol, ever polishing and improving their techniques in fighting Satan.

I recently got a text message from a young man who had to start over (go back to 0). He is a returned Missionary who has a girlfriend who he is very much in love with and wants to marry. He told me that his "lost battles" are the only thing keeping him from taking her to the temple.

I expressed concern that notwithstanding her being a supportive girlfriend, at some point, if he doesn't show signs of significant improvement, she will need to leave him for a man who can learn to win his battles instead of one who keeps "oopsing."

On further investigation, I learned that this young man is losing battles because he is not running to his flag pole when his fire alarms go off. Upon further exploration I learned that he does not do the drills of running to the flag pole unless he feels like it. He also revealed that sometimes he doesn't feel like it is necessary.

There are many verses of scripture that say things like, "By small and simple things are great things brought to pass" (Alma 37:6-7). The story of Naaman from the Old Testament (2 Kings 5:1-14) also validates this principle.

You will find as you read this book that many of the activities required to beat this addiction are small and simple and appear to lack value until you actually follow through on what is required.

Daily drills do many things for the brain. One of the most important is training the brain to do what it needs to do instead of doing what it feels like doing. We win battles because we need to, not because we feel like it.

Praying and Studying Daily

Every day, multiple times every day, our minds experience "hand grenades" and "cow pies". The dark side throws such ideas over the walls of our minds. He and his soldiers are relentless. Reading and listening to quality literature (primarily inspired literature) does several things for our minds. It strengthens our walls. It functions as a wall. (I almost always listen to the words of prophets, either modern or ancient as I fall asleep and as I wake up. I have observed that Satan likes to attack when I am half asleep in the morning or at night.) Reading and listening adds weapons to our arsenal. Refreshing our minds with these true principles makes it easier to fight off the lies that come at us from the Dark Side. It always amazes me when I work with a warrior who tries to get to 12 weeks and beyond without finding a way to read/listen every day. I know of no one who has succeeded for years without reading/listening almost every day. Just do it!

Analyzing Lost Battles

Question #5: "When you lost, what technique did the enemy use to defeat you?" "Is there a pattern?" "If you could replay the event, what could you have done to beat him?" "What drills can you do to make sure you win next time if he tries something similar?"

Analyzing lost battles is best done after questions 1-4 have been completed. In fact it is not uncommon to learn that the reason for the lost battle, if there has been any, are the result of a gap in the defense system addressed in the first four questions.

If there is still a question from the individual and/or the group as to why a young man had a lost battle, this is where the therapist really earns his money. It is his responsibility to accurately identify "what technique was used by the enemy" and train the whole group on how to win against that type of attack.

As I have studied other treatment programs, I have observed that quite often the participants feel encouraged to feel like there is something wrong with their character, and this is the cause of their "relapses". It has been my experience that any paradigm that causes the warrior to feel weaker or less confident, makes him more vulnerable to future lost battles. The chemicals that dominate the mind when a young man feels this way weaken him to further attack.

The chemical condition a young man must feel in order to win is associated with the feelings one experiences when he and his loved ones are under attack. This was previously described as Warrior Chemistry.

By carefully crafting the question, "When you lost, what technique did the *enemy* use to defeat you?" is intentionally intended to cause an almost automatic release of warrior chemistry. This increase in warrior chemistry sends cognitive energy into the cerebral cortex and the frontal lobe, empowering the young man to more accurately analyze what events and patterns led up to his most recent lost battle (or close call).

By processing the event backward, identifying the times, locations, thoughts and feelings associated with the different levels of the Chemical scale (5, 4, 3, 2, 1), the warrior can find patterns to what occurred. He can then replay the event, creating a plan of success along the way. Then he is encouraged to drill this plan over and over between this group session and the next.

Doing a "Q5": Analyzing Lost Battles

It is vital to analyze your lost battles correctly if you are going to be more prepared for the next attack. Usually, the process an untrained warrior goes through right after a lost battle is counterproductive. In typical situations, after a lost battle, the warrior feels significant guilt and self-loathing. Often he gets angry with himself and irritable with others. He feels stupid. He feels hopeless. Not much thinking takes place. If there is any thinking, it sounds something like, "Why was I so stupid?" Or, "What is wrong with me?" Because of this, most warriors try to forget the whole experience as fast as possible. The chemical shifting associated with these thoughts and feelings weaken the warrior and he becomes more susceptible to further lost battles. Spiritually, the young warrior has forgotten who he is and who he is up against.

A more healthy, useful and powerful approach can be observed in a military or athletic competition. I was a wrestler in high school. I took my sport pretty seriously. I was dedicated to winning my battles on the mat. It was nice to beat up on the guys who were not as skilled as I was, but important things happened in my heart and mind when I met a skilled opponent. As much as I don't want to admit it, there were times when I actually lost. The way I was coached to respond to these experiences has greatly impacted my research and training of young men who are fighting against Satan and his addictive behaviors.

As with sports, after a loss, a certain amount of anger and sadness is appropriate, if it builds the individual toward determination, instead of hopelessness. Imagine a military situation where because of some skill on the part of your enemy, one of your best friends gets killed right in front of you. If you stop and grieve for too long, it puts your own life in jeopardy. Sitting around crying and feeling stupid is just going to get you killed. So, how long should you feel like crud after a lost battle? Just long enough to be motivated to take the next step. This should take less than a few minutes.

It is valueless to linger in negative feelings toward one's opponent in sports. Many athletes lose some of their skill when they get consumed by negative feelings. It is more useful to gain an increase of respect for your opponent. You will notice that the question we use to train the young men is, ***"When you lost, what technique did the enemy use to defeat you?"*** This shifts the focus away from looking for weaknesses in the young man, and increases focus on the strengths of the opponent. I had no idea when I first started training men to beat addictions that they would need to gain a testimony of the power and intelligence of Satan, as fast as they were gaining a testimony of the power and intelligence of God.

With this new respect, laced with intense determination, the warrior will "review the video tapes". This is a very uncomfortable part of the process. Men do not like to be reminded what they do wrong. It is humiliating. But every serious athlete or performer must gain the courage to review their past if they are going to make the future better. When reviewing the 'video tapes', we look for patterns. ***"Is there a pattern?"***

In order to identify a pattern, it is wise to use the chemical scale as a reference and work your way backward.

Start with ***Level 5, the "I Give Up" moment,*** because analyzing anything after a level 5 is not a very valuable use of time. In order for an addict to succeed, he must watch for sensations in his body as accurately as possible. When a person experiencing addiction stops fighting against the temptation, "I Give Up" is the most common sensation experienced by the warrior.

After level 5, the higher brain is mostly numb and the body is just functioning like an animal. This is the moment in time when the warrior stops fighting and gives up (for the moment). I encourage the warrior to identify where he was (geographically) and at approximately what time he hit the "I Give Up" moment (within 15 minutes). The most common answer for beginners is, "I don't remember." I have learned that even blacking this out is part of the satanic strategy. If the warrior cannot "remember" how he got shot in the forehead, then he cannot prepare to avoid it in the future. With a bit of courage and concentration, the young man can identify his where and when.

Level 4, the Confused (Retarded) Conversation. I hope no one takes offense to my use of the word "retarded". I actually do know what it means scientifically, but so many of my clients can relate to this word better than all the others I have tried to use. To analyze a lost battle, we need to know how long the level 4 lasted, and what the conversation contained. Some have level 4 experiences that are barely a few seconds. Others can last days or months. "You know where this is headed. Yeah, I know. You should stop. Yeah, I know. Okay then, stop. Yeah okay..." until "I Give Up".

This phase is what most beginning warriors are referring to when they discuss fighting temptation. I sometimes refer to it as the "hand-to-hand combat" stage, because it is much harder to fight and win at this level than if you identify the attack and kill it from a distance (sniper shot), i.e. Level 1 or 2.

Level 3, the "Dude!" Moment. Every addict I have worked with understands this with minimal explanation. This is the first awareness of an inappropriate thought. It is one of the easiest parts of the scale to recognize. I encourage the warrior who has recently lost a battle to remember where and when he experienced the Dude! Moment. This can be seconds, minutes, hours, days, weeks, months, before the actual lost battle. While it is not most effective to fight battles at this level, it is helpful to be prepared. A warrior prepares by writing down as many "Dude's" as he can on paper, thus increasing the likelihood of identifying him (Satan) next time.

- "Dude, it has been a while."
- "Dude, your parents are gone. It is a perfect time."
- "Dude, you are going to lose eventually anyway, might as well do so now!"
- "Dude, your life sucks and isn't going anywhere anyway, might as well."
- Etc., etc., etc.

Level 3 is specifically designed to be a pain reliever. There is a "gate keeper" between the higher brain and the animal brain. One of the main jobs of the gate keeper is to propose solutions for pain when pain (emotional) becomes overbearing. The gate keeper has a handful of prepared activities based on what has worked in the past. When life becomes too _______, he says, "Dude..." Satan whispers to the gate keeper a suggestion that has worked in the past to relieve emotional pain, but usually does not take into consideration the values system.

Level 2, the Pain Build up. Feelings. In my experience, men of all ages are very uncomfortable with the idea of being pushed around by their own feelings. To avoid feeling like they are being influenced by feelings, they often just avoid being aware of having feelings. I know; I have done it myself! The build up from level 2 to level 3 is experienced when there is an increasing amount of legitimacy to one or more negative feelings.

For instance, if one of your Achilles' heel feelings is Overwhelm, then it might sound something like, "You are never going to get it all done. Expectations are too high. There isn't enough time. No one understands how much pressure this is." As the believability of the thoughts increase, the feelings increase. And an increase in negative feelings is associated with an increase in chemicals that make one vulnerable to satanic attacks. When Satan observes that there is probably enough emotional pain and vulnerability, the "Dude" moment occurs. This is when the animal brain, combined with some satanic assistance proposes an activity that will, "relieve the pressure."

Level 1, the first of the chemicals. As described before in the Satanic Spin, certain thoughts cause chemical reactions in the brain. The Satanic Spin specifically addresses the chemicals associated with deviant sexual behavior. Unfortunately, Satan is willing to manipulate other chemicals in your brain as well. To do so, he uses the same strategy. He carefully picks a thought that is likely to cause a chemical reaction in your brain. Any feeling that cannot be associated with what one can expect to feel in the presence of the Holy Ghost (peace, comfort, confidence, etc.) is associated with chemical reactions that increase animal brain activity and decrease higher brain functioning.

I remember for me there was a time when Satan could easily use, "You aren't going to have enough money to pay your bills this month." I remember waking up to this idea like a sucker punch in the gut. I remember the chemical spill in my body as I could feel my heart beating faster, and my mind starting to swirl. If I let such thoughts, and others like unto it continue to build, I could feel myself get more revved up, or spun. With careful observation I noticed my creative problem solving skills decrease and my moodiness increase. If I did not have the skills to diffuse the strong feelings, I can easily see how I would be increasingly inclined to do whatever it takes to eliminate the pain, even if it is not logical and not in agreement with my long term values.

So, ***to analyze your own lost battle***, review:

- Where and when did you say, "I Give Up"? (Level 5)
- Where and when did you experience the "Retarded Conversation"? (Level 4)
    - What were some of the thoughts associated with this phase?
- Where and when do you remember the first "Dude" moment? (Level 3)
- Where and when did you start to believe the strong negative feelings that were spilling into your mind? (Level 2)
    - Which negative feelings built up the pain this time?
- Where and when did you first get informed of a negative feeling? (Level 1)
    - What thought(s) initiated this feeling?
- Is there a pattern to the times, locations, feelings and thoughts?

"If you could replay the event, what could you have done to beat him?"

As with sports and military situations, finding patterns in the methods of your opponent make it much easier to beat him. If you know that a military enemy is always going to hide in your bedroom at night and try to stab you with a knife as you are trying to fall asleep, how do you defeat him? Sounds pretty simple when you put it that way, huh? It has been my experience that about 90% of all "lost battles" take place at predictable times in predictable locations.

Example: Here is a common military strategy I have seen Satan use on our young men. The young man is on his way home from a long day at work or school. He is reminded of how hard he has been working and the thought of any more work in this moment could ruin his life, so he *needs* some "down time". Feelings of overwhelm or overwork start increasing the closer he gets to home. "Dude" moments start to occur, not about misbehaviors at first, but behaviors that put the young man in a more vulnerable position, like TV, or a nap in his room. As the young man's brain remembers how much more there is to do that day (homework, chores, etc.) the pain increases. Eventually, the need for an even bigger "release" is present and the official "Dude" moment occurs. A little argument...and then...crash. (Try to identify the 1, 2, 3, 4, 5 of this paragraph.)

So, after identifying the 1, 2, 3, 4, 5, create a plan to be a step ahead in the 1-2 zone. You must notice the moment in time when you feel a *need* to do something to resolve the strong negative feelings that are building. You must have a pre-created plan that will rejuvenate the body and mind accurately. You remember that watching TV actually does not rejuvenate the body and mind. But a vigorous sport for a reasonable amount of time does work (basketball, running, biking, etc.). Then get right on your stewardships (homework, chores) so you can finish the day with a sense of manly satisfaction, instead of another negative feeling of avoiding manly responsibilities.

If your 1-2 zone is in the area of stress, then you need to gain the skills of stress management. When Satan uses stress, he builds upon the idea that you will never be able to get it all done, have enough money, etc. With depression he builds upon "legitimate" descriptions of your flaws or hopelessness in life. The possibilities are endless, but in our favor, in most cases we each only have about 3 major "Achilles' heel" emotions. You may need some extra training on how to identify and how to create effective mood management skills, but once an effective plan is created...

"What drills can you do to make sure you win next time if he tries something similar?"

It is not uncommon that the final mistake I see warriors make is here. They think it is a good idea to have a plan, but they don't come up with one that will actually work. A good plan must include what you will do differently once you identify each Level. In other words, "How will you recognize and what will you do if you feel the same Level 2"? "What will you do, instantly, if you hear the same "Dude, moment?" Etc.

Another error is that they come up with an effective plan, but then don't practice it when they are NOT under attack. In all three comparative activities, music, sports and military, there is actual practice - WITH THE BODY - in artificial situations BEFORE the actual event is experienced. If you are going to defeat a skilled enemy, you MUST practice, practice, practice! You must get your body to the point where it will take the necessary action quickly and without having to think about it.

For instance, the young warrior who discovers that he is regularly attacked right after school, and decides that going out to play basketball before working on other things, must do this every day, even if he doesn't think it is necessary. Imagine telling a boot camp instructor that you didn't do the drills that were needed because you didn't FEEL like it! So many "Lost battles" begin with losing an "I don't feel like it" battle over a necessary drill. The young men I work with who go on to succeed learn to respond with "Do it anyway" to every emotional excuse I propose to them to shirk drills.

If your 1-2 zone is stress, then every day at your vulnerable time you do your relaxation drills. If your 1-2 zone is depression, then you review your confidence building concepts that are written out on 3x5 cards at your vulnerable time.

If you really, really, want to learn how to beat this addiction, then you will type up the 4 parts of Question 5, and answer them in detail as guided above. I highly recommend you answer the questions EVERY time you have a lost battle. The process is difficult, but it will do wonders for your brain.

The next chapter contains a section entitled, "What Went Wrong". This is a play-by-play analysis of some lost battles for you to learn from:

Question #6: "What might the enemy try in the future?" "What do you need to do to be prepared for such an attack?"

As you might guess, one of the most painful moments in time for both me, the clinician, and my warrior client, is when he or she is doing so well, then "out of no-where" they are attacked and lose a battle. After a great deal of pondering and prayer, I was listening to a story from the Book of Mormon and got the following revelation.

Alma 16 tells the story of a military leader, Zoram, who visits Alma asking him how to prepare for the future. In verse 6, Alma inquires of the Lord and is told where and when the enemy will be. After listening to this story, the concept came to mind, "Teach them to prophesy." It might surprise you to find out that at that time, ***I*** did not know how to prophesy! I went on to discover that it is not nearly as complicated as I once thought, and it can be taught, even to teenagers!

In preparation for the up and coming week/day/hour, the young men are trained to ask God to help them see when, where and how the Enemy is going to attack next. Then, the warrior needs to ponder (think after praying) and prophesy (guess with the Spirit) when and where the next Satanic attack will take place. Many are surprised that this takes less effort than expected, but it does take enough effort to at least try. The warrior must first pray for assistance. Then he considers the schedule for the upcoming period of time. He then identifies the few times and locations of likely attacks. This is best done if it is narrowed down to one or two 15 minute time slots. To be more successful, the warrior will need to identify each of the 5 Levels as they build up. Again, this is done best by working backward. Most of the warriors are surprised by their own accuracy.

After identifying the most likely time and location for the next attack, they prepare a plan to dominate, instead of "slip". If the warrior finds that they will need specific assistance from God, now is the time to ask for that as well.

"Help me to remember…" and "Please provide me with…" are two of the more effective ways to pray. They then practice this plan either in their minds or in real time (as would an athlete or a soldier) including the emotion of the event. With sufficient preparation, the warrior can and will succeed!

With practice, warriors go on to win for many years. They learn that by aligning themselves with the power of God, there is no strategy or attack that Satan can surprise them with that is too much for them to handle.

As they align themselves with the power of God, they are also aligning themselves with God's ministering angel warriors. They experience something similar to what the young man experienced in the story with Elisha found in 2 Kings 6:15-17.

"And when the servant of the man of God was risen early, and gone forth, behold, an host (army) compassed (surrounded) the city both with horses and chariots. And his servant said unto him (Elisha), Alas, my master! how shall we do?

"And he answered, Fear not: for **they that be with us are more than they that be with them**.

"And Elisha prayed, and said, Lord, I pray thee, open his eyes, that he may see. And the Lord opened the eyes of the young man; and he saw: and, behold, the mountain was full of horses and chariots of fire round about Elisha "(emphasis added).

Warriors learning to plan and prepare against Satan's attacks can pray to have their spiritual eyes opened and see the angelic forces ailing them in this battle for their souls.

Chapter 10

What Went Wrong

Common Mistakes made by those who have not yet perfected the art of fighting against an addiction.

Every day in group, warriors answer the Captain's Log questions. I am excited every time we arrive at question 5 (Q5 as we often refer to it in group): "When you lost, what technique did the enemy use to defeat you? Is there a pattern?" I get excited because answering this question provides me with some of the best opportunities to teach Satan's methodology. Analyzing lost battles is an extremely helpful part of group therapy, not only does the defeated warrior learn how to win next time, but every other warrior in the group comes away knowing better how to defend themselves from Satan's attacks. I found this approach so successful; I decided to dedicate an entire chapter to illustrating some examples.

If you are struggling with an addiction, pay special attention to these lost battles and think what *you* might do in these situations to prevent yourself from falling prey to the enemy's traps. During these analyses, the client's words are italicized and my comments are in normal font.

Example #1:
The Gradual Descent

"Somehow, out of the business that is my life now, I lost another battle. I woke up extremely early this morning and I could not get back to sleep."

This is Level 1: The Chemical Spill. The addict brain, with the help of Satan, can set off alarms that mechanically shift chemicals that wake you up in order to get a "fix". It is wise to remember that this experience is a legitimate addiction, not unlike heroin. With all addictions there are withdrawal symptoms. Waking up in the middle of the night and not being able to go back to sleep is a common withdrawal symptom. This will usually go away after about 3 weeks of success.

"Within what seemed like two hours of idly waiting for sleep to come to me..."

This is Level 2: Feelings. In an effort to understand why we woke up, or why we can't go back to sleep, uncomfortable, pre-sexual feelings increase with the help of the Satanic Spin. Sleep will not just "come to you" in these situations. The warrior must intentionally change his brain chemistry. A burst of exercise will often do the trick. It is important that he takes the necessary course of action before he gets to Level 3.

"...temptation reared its ugly head."

This is Level 3: The Dude Moment. The first suggestion to do something inappropriate. Now his brain has been massaged into vulnerability.

"I eventually went upstairs."

This is Level 4: The Retarded Conversation. "Should I? Should I not? Etc."

"...and started to surf the internet for bad material."

This is Level 5: The "I Give Up" Moment. The addict stops fighting it, decides to let go of the reigns and lets the stallions of his passion run away with his moral stagecoach.

"I can't handle vulgar material for too long before my mind begins to try and purge it, so I turned off the computer and left feeling guilty and dirty."

At this point, we are in Damage Control. It is almost too late for the warrior to win this battle. Decisions have to be made in advance in order to maintain the fewest "casualties" in each lost battle.

"I lost a battle to masturbation before I left for band camp. I had rationalized that after the loss to pornography, 'If you lose to masturbation now, there will be no way you can convince yourself you are still worthy to bless the sacrament.'"

This is another visit to Levels 3, 4 and 5 before the warrior returned back to 0. I assume the addict can recognize the lack of logic in this sentence now that he is out of the situation and thinking straight again.

"I often had the question, 'how far is too far' with Mr. P?"

Question 5, part 3 from Captain's Log: This is a good question. I recommend a warrior move his standard up to a line to only viewing things he would watch with his mother sitting next to him. This will put his standards where they need to be in preparation for a mission and marriage in the temple. It seems a little strict, but it will relieve his conscience of all obnoxious conversations about "maybes", which can sometimes be a foothold for justification and indulgence.

"I have not yet gotten to directly searching for the worst of it, but I am getting closer and closer to that point. I think it would be for the best if I restrict the internet better for areas I have access to."

Computer/internet restrictions are wise, but insufficient if you are going to beat this stuff for a lifetime. To win forever, you draw a line in the sand in a very safe place, and then fight for it with all ferocity.

"I need to be more aware of lurking temptation. I also think that I need to be more diligent in responding to texts in the Text-Coaching program."

This is a good analysis. Those who are faithful in their accountability system, like Text Coaching, tend to succeed faster. In Text Coaching, answering *every* question in a timely manner is the key to its success.

"I need to not let my guard down at any time and plan ahead for situations like today's."

Yes, most of us can predict with some degree of accuracy where and when Satan will attack. That is the point of Question 6 from the Captain's Log. Planning an activity that will dominate the Adversary in advance will greatly increase your success.

Example #2
A "Surprise" Attack

"Today was a stupid loss. "

Right off the bat, he is attributing to himself weakness, instead of attributing to Satan strength and intelligence.

"It was not what I intended today."

Recognition that he was in an altered state of mind – what we call "Stoned".

"From start to finish it was over in 5 minutes. "

Level 5: I Give Up – Nothing really to talk about at this point.

"5 minutes is all it takes to ruin my building momentum."

It is very important how the warrior responds to a loss of momentum. There are two categories of emotion the warrior could experience with the awareness of having momentum lost. As with an athlete, if he starts to feel hopeless, or self-deprecating, he will start to fall apart. If he is aware of the skills of an opponent, he can become ferociously determined to figure out what the opponent was able to put together in the form of a strategy, and create an even more amazing strategy – combine it with focused ferocity and go on to dominate.

This client has a tendency to be very responsible, perhaps even *overly* responsible. It never ceases to amaze me how Satan will take advantage of either end of a personality spectrum. Satan will easily manipulate a person who avoids responsibility, but he can also work on the overly responsible person. This is unexpected by some people, and when it is unexpected, it falls into the "The serpent was the most subtle of all the beasts of the field" category.

In this case, this overly responsible warrior is taking ALL the credit for his lost battles and is not giving Satan credit for his role in the battle. If this warrior will give Satan credit, he will remember to look for the Level 1 phase. He needs to increase his Spirit of Discernment to look for his subtle biochemical shifts and his emotional condition. Like most men (as you will see below), he is attending to his actions (Level 5) and to some degree his thoughts (Level 3). He recently sent me a very good write up on fighting battles. This write up is good, but it still does not attend to the 2 most basic elements of fighting this war – the satanic factor, and the chemical factor. Let's read on:

"I had written a detailed plan of how I was going to win 12 days in a row. Just 12 days. The goal is a modest one.
I had a detailed plan for how my mornings would go and how I would win.

"Last night I went trick or treating with the family I used to work for. I was a little annoyed to have to drive to a different city."

This is a Level 2. It is good that he noticed it, but he did not give it sufficient credit. He then mentions why he was annoyed.

"I was hoping to go food shopping and finish organizing my room. But the visit was a good one. I am glad that I went."

It appears that his emotions and chemicals balanced out.

"I made it home on time, I wrote a brief but solid letter to my future wife. I have been writing those since early August. I like to review the day, my feelings, and a little bit about how I will win the next day. I suppose it was a bit rushed and not as thorough as it could have been.

"This morning I got up on time and had plenty of time to get ready. I decided to drive and not ride the train so I had time to lay in my bed and read the Book of Mormon."

I don't know if this warrior has ever noticed how unwise it is to read in bed in the morning, but I would read this as a mix of good with bad, a common satanic strategy.

"I read 1 Nephi 22. I had a brilliant revelation. I was reading verse 26 and it speaks of the millennium. Satan will be bound not because he will be locked up and cast out but BECAUSE OF THE RIGHTEOUSNESS OF THE PEOPLE.

"I had the idea that Satan can be bound in terms of beating me because I will pay no attention to him and his temptations. Maurice has been doing this for years."

I am glad he wrote this because it reveals an inaccurate understanding which many young men have a hard time understanding—in fact many not-so-young men struggle understanding this. If we are Nephites in Book of Mormon times, we cannot afford to "pay no attention" to the Lamanites. We must actively watch for and prepare for them. I use the almost constant listening to the words of the prophets primarily as "walls" to protect my mind, but also as a forge for new weapons. Also, this listening trains me in the ways of both the power of God and the power of Satan, so I can fight with precision.

"Even as I drove to work I listened to a book on CD that discusses the atonement. I was feeling pretty dang good. Perhaps I was getting a little too confident. I got to work early. About 10 minutes. I guess it isn't good to be too early because that means I am alone before anyone else gets there. I was hoping to check email and maybe send some emails to friends before the official work day began."

Good efforts, but notice in his analysis, he is still primarily discussing his actions, and not his feelings/mood (Level 2s) or chemical shifts (Level 1s). Again, I would venture to say, his Spirit of Discernment has not yet been sharpened enough to sense these things.

"I got an email update from Amazon. I order good books on Amazon every now and then."

He is now wandering aimlessly. Think like a sniper in a war. Is there ever an option to drop your guard? Perhaps we resent the need to be so vigilant. I remind my clients, people who were born into battle zones do not have a choice and they do not take time to resent it. They learn that you must do what you have to do, or you are dead.

"Today, the spirit faintly poked me not to click on the link. I did anyway."

Here he is already at Level 4, and too stoned to fight back.

"My brain seemed to be a bit automatic. As I was looking at some of the books that were recommended based on what I had done before. The temptation hit me to click on the clothing link for women's intimate apparel."

Here he has a second Level 3 "Dude" Moment.

"The rest is sort of history at that point. It was all over pretty quick. Full act out. Dang it!! I knew I had blown my goal. I went to the bathroom to clean up and also to pray. That was a stupid loss."

Self-deprecation – not helpful.

"It seems that I lose often in the mornings. I realize that checking email right at 7 a.m. is probably not a good idea. I will make it a goal not to start clicking on email or any links that are not specifically for work for the first hour."

Where is the conversation about the involvement of Satan? Have you been tricked into believing that this is a war between your Spirit self and your Body self, and there are no other intelligent participants? One of the important questions in the Captain's Log is carefully crafted, "When you lost, <u>what technique did the enemy use to defeat you</u>?" You will notice that this does not say, "When you lost, what did you do wrong?" Self-loathing and frustration are two strong emotions that Satan wants to stimulate within us. Those two emotions and any emotions like unto them involve chemicals that make the brain more vulnerable/susceptible to future attacks. Anger at self is not productive "a house divided against itself cannot stand". We must focus our anger/fighting energy outward – toward the actual culprit. We must gain a testimony of our own goodness – we would never pick self-destruction for ourselves by choice. We will only choose it when an outside force suggests it and distorts us to the point where we consider it both attractive and of sufficient value to pursue.

"I respond to a text (<u>Text Coaching</u>) at 7:20 and I have an alarm at 9 p.m. I will not even log on to the computer until I have read my oath and said a prayer. If I do this for the next few weeks, it will become a habit. Maybe I will get in the habit of completely closing down my computer every evening so that in the morning it will be obvious when I come in the morning to prepare myself.
I will put a post it note on my mouse every evening that will remind me to pray and prepare in the morning.

"This losing at work business is ridiculous. This could lead to some major disasters.

"Today, I am going to work extra effective. I will work out at lunch. I will organize this Saturday's dinner group and contact the people in the group. I will email and possibly call the girls. It will help my brain to take charge and do that.

"After work, I will go food shopping. In the evening I want to read some good articles on addiction that I found on a site by a recovered addict. I will read some of step 1 and 2 of the 12 steps. Tonight will be a regeneration night. I will still finish out the week. I will prepare extra carefully. I will write a long letter to wife (30 minutes) and describe how it is that I lost. I will make a better plan for Wednesday. I am going to take a girl out to lunch tomorrow.

"This was a stupid loss and there are probably more complicated things going on inside of me, but I still want to stay true to my battle plan, keep border patrol tight, vigilance at all hours of the day, rely on God, and win every day until Sunday. There is no other option.

"Oh, and tomorrow I am going to go to SA at 6 a.m. It will be worth it. I want to be committed to going every week rain or snow!!!"

The planning of his actions is impressive, but he has not identified times and locations where he is probably going to be in the zone between Levels 1-3: Chemical, Feeling/Mood increase. If this warrior is going to win in the future, he is going to have to move the battlefield to these more sensitive regions. He is a smart man. He is skilled with action. So it does not surprise me that he tries to fight where he is strong. Unfortunately, all warriors are going to have to learn how to fight on all levels. The enemy has changed his attack strategy to a level we never before thought possible. If he is going to hit the basic elements of our body chemistry, we cannot ignore it.

Example #3
Putting Your Alarms in the Wrong Place

"Maurice, here is question 5 after my lost battle last night.

"The technique used was with my iPod. This is the same technique Satan has used in my last lost battles. Like this last battle, my previous lost battle 56 days ago, he used my pride against me. I felt adequately strong enough in my own efforts to bypass the border patrol that had kept me alive in the last 8 weeks.

I downloaded an app that slowly tempted me here and there till I gave in. It was late at night when it took place, in my room. This is the same pattern.

"Level 5 in the 'I Give Up' stage felt like it never came. It continually felt like a retarded conversation. The reality of level 5 occurred when YouTube just wasn't working for me, so I downloaded a google app. (I, till the day before, had it so I could not download apps onto my iPod and YouTube was also blocked-for this reason.)"

This is a good analysis so far, but in order to be thorough, we would need to look for the I Give Up moment associated with changing the setting on the iPod that allows you to download apps. If there was a legitimate app that you needed, then we need to discuss why you didn't follow through on resetting the settings to blocking downloads.

"Level 4 was during YouTube and specifically right before deciding to download the other app.

"Level 3 was after a long and tiring night at work. As I got out of my car and grabbed my iPod the 'dude' came. I shrugged off that feeling and had the thought to perhaps leave my iPod there in the car overnight. After this thought I sat in my car for a minute listening to music then grabbed my iPod out of habit and went inside feeling stronger than I really was to overcome the temptations that were to follow."

Notice how you are convoluting thoughts and feelings. In order to win this war, you are going to have to not only move your alarm system from the Level 3 (thoughts) beyond the Level 2 (feelings) to the fine point of Level 1 (chemicals). As with any military strategy, confusing the enemy with something like smoke bombs is an important technique. If you cannot isolate the elements of the attack, you will not be able to kill it.

Notice that the "dude" moment is a thought. In your analysis there is no description of feelings. You did use one feeling word in your Level 2 analysis, but you have almost no feeling words in this analysis. I understand (and can relate) that, as a man, noticing feelings, let alone naming them can be very challenging. If I were to guess what you are feeling in the car it would be some kind of agitation. Feelings associated with thoughts like, "I don't care. I don't want restrictions" (frustrated with needing restrictions/rules). I want to relax and stop thinking" (feeling tension and/or overwhelmed). There could be aggravation associated with feeling like you aren't where you want to be in life and things aren't going the way you had planned.

You may be feeling stress because you are behind and you don't feel like you are catching up.

In future analysis, work hard to find at least 5 feelings associated with each lost battle (or close call). You may need to pray for the Spirit of Discernment before doing this. You may need to do some guessing. You may need a thesaurus.

With respect to "went inside feeling stronger than I really was", while it is true that we can only have one thought at a time, we can have more than one feeling at a time. We can feel confident and worried at the same time. And remember, even drunk drivers do not think they are too drunk to drive.

"Level 2 was still lurking from a level 3 and almost 4 earlier in the day (Satan using the same technique then as in this lost battle). I was bored at home knowing that I did not need to get up early the next day and was wanting something entertaining to do at the late hour after work.

"Level 1 came, as I said, from work being long and tiring and annoying with lots to do, not enough time to do it and no energy to want to work. Plus because there was so much to do, I missed my ward FHE get together."

This is good, but now name the feelings associated with missing the FHE get together.

If you look closely, with the Spirit of Discernment, you will be able to identify physiological feelings associated with your body more than your emotions. If you look closely, you will be aware of a change in your breathing, a slight shift in your pores (almost sweating if not already doing so). Notice the pace of your heart rate.

In order to win for a life time, you will need to memorize and "bookmark" the elements of your Level 1 and Level 2. You will need to attach an alarm (trip wire) to these feelings. That trip wire is going to have to be connected to your Warrior Chemistry bucket. You will need to respond with the same intensity that you would if you heard someone sneaking into your baby daughter's bedroom in the middle of the night with a knife to slit her throat!

"Replaying the event, I see many places where I could have countered Satan's attacks. When downloading the google app I could have stopped there. I could have listened to the prompting of leaving my iPod in my car. But the biggest thing I could have done is not leaving the gaping hole in my border by allowing myself to be able to download apps and allowing YouTube on my iPod. That had been my safety in times of winning and this same mistake has been the reason of my falls. Satan used my pride of the number of weeks to destroy me when I was literally a week away from going back to the temple – for the first time in at least 6 months."

Your ideas are valiant, but too late. You have listed 3 behaviors/actions you need to attend to. If I were Satan, I would just smile. It is almost like you plan is to duck faster next time you hear a bomb going off. As we all know, if you hear the sound of a bomb, it is already too late. We need to get you to the point where you are like a dog and you can smell bombs. We need you to be able to sense the presence of bombs and then to react with the same intensity.

"Drills I shall implement are, for one, asking my mom to follow up with me when I ask her to unlock my restrictions on my iPod so she can re-lock whatever it was I was wanting to do or download in the first place, eliminating that chance for Satan to slip in through the wide open door with a welcome sign on it."

Another valiant effort, but there are two major pieces that need to be corrected:

1. Don't make a plan that relies on another person. People may love us, but they have their own burdens to bear, and they may not be in a position to help in the time of crisis. The verse, "do not rely upon the arm of flesh" comes to mind. If someone is there to help, that is a bonus. We need to make a plan that does not require another person's help.

2. Your plan does not include actual Drills. Drills are things you do over and over and over again. There will need to be some similarity to military, athletic or music training if it is going to classify as a real drill. Drills in sports often include a pattern of, "They do this, then we do this, then they do this, then we do this, etc." Drills are initially done in slow motion, and then sped up to real time. Drills are done over and over and over again until they become automatic.

In your situation, with this type of Satanic attack, I would first get very clear on the initial physiological sensations (Level 1) and emotions (Level 2) commonly experienced in this location (car/bedroom) at this time of day (end of a long day). Then I would make a plan to feel (dump warrior chemistry into my body – sometimes referred to as the "Oh, Shoot!" moment). Then I would bust out of my car/bedroom and run full speed out to my mailbox or the nearest stop sign as if someone I love is being attacked in that location.

Then I would go back to my original place, remember/call to mind my Level 1 and Level 2 sensations, dump the Warrior Chemicals again and sprint to the same "Flag Pole" again with the same intensity. I would do this 5 times every day for 21 days. If you really want to beat this addictive behavior for the rest of your life, you will have to do whatever it takes. If you are hoping you will not have to get this dedicated or this ferocious, I invite you to remember Mosiah 20:11 "...and like Dragons did they fight!"

You can use the same system to overpower the "I don't feel like doing my border patrol" sensations. Go to the place where you tend to have that feeling. Recall the feeling (Satan's attack), then crush his head with your body, with Warrior Chemistry and sprinting to your "Flag Pole". Do this 5 times a day for 21 days and every time you "don't feel like" border patrolling. Soon you will scare that feeling right out of your system.

For more examples of Analyzing Lost Battles [Q5s], go to www.mwHarkerTherapist.blogspot.com.

Chapter 11

Graduation

How do I maintain success after the intense 12 week training?

Congratulations on completing 12 weeks! But your fight isn't over yet, you still have the rest of your life to prove yourself as the powerful warrior and Son of God you are. You will have many battles ahead of you. If you continue to overcome them, you will become stronger.

Many warriors hope that there will come a day that the battles will be over. My response is to remind the warrior of what he learned from the Book of Mormon. "When will the Lamanites stop attacking the Nephites?" Continued battles have nothing to do with the level of righteousness of the warrior. Continued battles will occur because of the personality of the enemy. As long as the warrior is a threat to Satan, he may be fighting until the day he dies. It would be unwise to ever put your guard down. You cannot afford to lose again! There are many who rely on you to protect them.

In this chapter, I will cover 5 lessons every Sons of Helaman graduate should remember throughout his life to effectively combat Satan and come off victorious.

Lesson 1: Stay Humble

"I give unto men weakness that they may be humble; and my grace is sufficient for all men that humble themselves before me; for if they humble themselves before me, and have faith in me, then will I make weak things become strong unto them." Ether 12:27

You have become humble and full of faith to beat this problem. However, you are strong not because you can handle satanic attacks on your own, but because you are disciplined to keep yourself aligned with God. Notice how the word "discipline" is much like the word "disciple". A disciple follows one God. And has once been said, you cannot build a mansion in heaven and keep a summer home in Babylon.

President Thomas S. Monson counsels us this way:

"Many movies and television shows portray behavior which is in direct opposition to the laws of God. Do not subject yourself to the innuendo and outright filth which are so often found there" ("Priesthood Power," April 2011 General Conference, Priesthood session).

His counsel is clear and his language strong: "outright filth". Any show that causes those deviant sex chemicals to flow is not appropriate for any church member to watch, especially you. The same way a recovering alcoholic doesn't drink even a little bit. Sometimes you will have to make personal sacrifices, but you will be strengthened and blessed. Is it really worth it to watch a lewd movie your friends suggest, bringing back those same chemicals you were in bondage to? Would you become re-addicted rather than sacrificing a little bit of your social standing? Do not let pleasing your friends endanger your cleanliness.

A good idea would be to remember what you've learned. This battle has caused you to learn a great deal about God and His mercies, the Savior's atonement, and the patterns of Satan. Write them down in a journal or in a letter to a fellow warrior. You have also learned a great deal about yourself, how you react in different situations, why you have certain behaviors, what bothers you, and probably quite a bit about how to recognize your feelings.

Take these skills and use them. They will help you a lot in fighting this tremendous battle for the rest of your life.

Lesson 2: Go To War Against Satan

"How can I prevent myself from falling back into this addiction?" The recent graduate will ask himself. "Will I be strong enough?" "Will I fall into Satan's traps again?" "What can I do to prevent this?"

Alma the Younger, after receiving the mighty change in his heart, described what he did to keep that change:

"Yea, and from that time until now, I have labored without ceasing, that I might bring souls to repentance; that I might bring them to taste of the exceeding joy of which I did taste; that they might be born of God, and be filled with the Holy Ghost" (Alma 36:24).

Alma defended his new self by launching an all-out offensive against Satan. He didn't just say, "Phew, I'm glad I got that off my back, now I can get back to normal life." "Normal life" is just the first step to complacency and slipping up. We can't go back to normality; we have to take a stand. We have to fight for others now.

The 12th step in Alcoholics Anonymous reads:

"Having had a spiritual awakening as a result of these Steps, we tried to carry this message to others, and to practice these principles in all our affairs."

This is not just a weak acknowledgment of indebtedness, *"I guess I should help someone else since I was helped, maybe I owe it to them."* Rather this is our call to arms, and the very key to our long-term success.

The most successful graduates from Sons of Helaman are those who have directed their knowledge and energy gained from the program and learned to "practice these principles in all [their] affairs." If they are of age, they throw themselves into fatherhood and being good husbands with the force they previously used to win battles. Work and church callings take on a new light; they are now fighting to free others, and everywhere they look for someone to help and lift. The weapons of war we used to fight Satan can be used as tools of healing to "lift up the hands which hang down, and strengthen the feeble knees" (D&C 81:5).

There is a powerful awareness group called "Fight the New Drug." This organization raises awareness of pornography and its addicting power. This is a great way to become involved in fighting Satan and pornography. Look it up online: www.fightthenewdrug.org. Get information on events and how to help spread the word (and to give the Sons of Helaman a good review on the resources page while you are at it). FTND can act as an automatic passion project. You may play a role in helping some people from ever starting down this dangerous path.

Graduating from Sons of Helaman (going 12 consecutive weeks without any lost battles) isn't the end. It's just the beginning. It begins a new level of warfare: our spiritual D-Day.

Lesson 3: Serve a Mission

One great way to go to war against Satan is to serve a full time mission; if you haven't already, you need to go. You have experiences and a testimony that have come from your specific challenges that the Lord can use to bless His children. You have learned about how much the atonement can be applied to anyone, no matter how bad the sins have been. There are people who wonder if they can be forgiven of their sins, but you know they can because you've experienced that yourself.

Go! Teach them! You are going to love it! Ask anyone who went on a mission after struggling with this problem. They have been more mature and effective missionaries. But it is always wise to be properly prepared.

According to many young men who went on missions after graduating from this program, it's very worth it to be prepared. Although it may be harder or the social pressure may be great, be sure you're ready. You probably won't have a problem on your mission, but afterward, if you didn't have it beat in regular life for a few months, you will probably have a very difficult time. It will be much better for you to know how to handle this addiction in everyday life.

If you are 17 or older ask to join *Sons of Mosiah*. This is a confidential email support group that we created at Sons of Helaman designed to support those who are pre, post and current missionaries. The Sons of Mosiah program is also for missionaries who are having lost battles and never had a chance to go through Sons of Helaman before going on missions. If you know of someone in this unfortunate position, get them enrolled ASAP.

Lesson 4: Do Not Stop As An RM

What should you do after your mission? A lot of guys who graduated and went on missions came back and Satan slammed them. It's very likely this will happen to you. What to do about it?

(1) Enroll in Sons of Mosiah right away (see previous page). The combination of helping others at the same time as being accountable to them is irreplaceable.

(2) Be prepared. Have an action plan, have a border patrol. Find your triggers or dangerous ground and plan on how you can stay away from them.

(3) Go to groups. You can come back as a General and help your brothers in battle. Tell of your experiences and how the group helped you prepare for a mission.

(4) Find a passion project. This will help direct the passion and energy you will gain from the mission, it will help keep you out of trouble, and it will help you become a creator, a dreamer, and a passionate man.

(5) Start looking for your eternal companion. This means dating. It will help you keep your emotions going in a positive way, and you'll be relating to young women in a positive way (much more positive than with your old buddies masturbation and pornography). Plus the young women you date will be a source of strength to you and the goal of temple marriage will help you in difficult moments. You will probably really make a mess of dating for the first year home from your mission, but that is okay, we all need time to learn things, including how to have healthy relationships.

Also, when you find that special young lady, make sure that before you get too far you tell her about your previous addiction. It may possibly cause her heartache, but if she is the one she will be understanding and forgive you. Your honesty will build trust and you will be able to rely on her if there are ever any slip ups in the future. You need to have no secrets from your future spouse. In most cases, sharing generalized information increases the depth and connection of your relationship.

You do not have to tell every girl right away, but if you become serious, do not wait too long. If you're in doubt, counsel with the Lord on the best time. Think about when you would want your 20 year old daughter to know about the history of the men she dates. I use the phrase, "tell her right before she falls in love with you."

(6) Attend the temple, and maybe even do some family history research. You'll receive great strength as you attend the temple regularly. It will help you maintain sensitivity as well so you can see Satan coming from a distance before he gets in your face.

(7) Keep setting goals. Don't be like a lot of returned missionaries that go to college and bum around without any goals or direction in life. You have a connection with your Father in Heaven. Build and strengthen that by setting worthy goals with Him about school, work, dating, church activity, etc.

(8) Do your daily border patrol. Make sure you regularly evaluate the effectiveness of your Border Patrol activities. This is one of the most powerful ways of staying away from temptation. It may change a lot after your mission—your border patrol may be simply doing scripture study and prayers. Just always, *ALWAYS* make sure it is enough to give you the strength and sensitivity to win. Never let go of the iron rod by reading/listening to the words of the prophets modern and old, every day.

(9) Seek support from your bishop. Tell your bishop about your previous issues, and don't be afraid to talk to him if you have a relapse. Your bishop is a great source of support (and you can also refer him to the Sons of Helaman if he has any other guys struggling with this addiction).

(10) Don't Forget. Lastly, *do not forget this counsel after two years in the mission field.* Make sure you take this counsel seriously.

Lesson 5: Stay in Touch

Here at Sons of Helaman, we are dedicated to making sure that you continue to defeat Satan all throughout your life. We hope you know that. We are here for you and have created several ways that graduates can stay in touch even as they move forward with life.

Letters. ". . . and when thou art converted, strengthen thy brethren." (Luke 22:32). You've defeated Satan with the help of the tools and tricks learned in Sons of Helaman. You are going to want to share some of the things you have learned with new warriors. We have on our website testimonials/trainings of warriors who completed the group. We want yours. You are invited to write a letter and send it to us. Address your letter to the guy who is currently too scared to get the training he needs.

Contact Information. Please keep us updated with your current contact information. This allows us to inform you of upcoming events or activities, and to be able to periodically check up and make sure you are receiving the help you need to keep winning. Fighting Satan is a life-long battle, and we will be with you for the long-haul. We would love to keep you on our emailing list and texting lists, so keep us with an updated email and phone number (preferably cell).

Conclusion

"I promise to be of service to you, and I will allow you to be of service to me, until both you and I successfully defeat this Demon that assails us."

Chapter 12

Prevention

As the Sons of Helaman™ program has grown, many parents have approached me with that intense look that only a protective parent can give and have asked, "Maurice, thank you for what you have done for my son, but what do you have for my younger son (or my husband) to help him keep from getting caught in this trap? Sometimes it seems hopeless." For all you wonderful mothers and fathers out there, know that prevention is possible. After a great deal of observation and research, I have been able to find the element of dysfunction that makes an individual susceptible to addiction. This element of functioning is not permanent and one can be trained to overcome and overpower it. If a parent wants a thorough training on how to train their children to be able to avoid slipping into the bondage of addiction my highest recommendation is the Eternal Warriors™ prevention program.

Since most of us like to try to do things on our own at home before seeking professional training, below is a discussion on pre-addiction psychology in young men, and a few small interventions you might try.

"How do I discuss sexuality without creating curiosity that ends up backfiring on me?"

Is Fire Good or Bad?

Using a "fire" analogy with young men helps them to conceptualize what they are dealing with without over-sexualizing the conversation. I ask them this question, "Is fire good or bad?" The usual, and right answer is, "It depends." We go on to discuss when it is good and when it is bad.

The conversation easily transitions into something like this: *There is a fire inside you that is going to grow over time. If you keep it the right size and in the right place, it will provide you with comfort and warmth. If you let it grow too big, (e.g., scout camp fires), it could destroy many things.*

Here I must add a disclaimer: preventing a son's exposure to negative sexual influences is ***almost*** impossible, and addiction is becoming ever more common. Satan has unleashed his degrading powers on the earth and sexual content is virtually everywhere. Also, the male brain is very powerfully affected by sexual content. It is unlikely that you will be able to keep him from ever being exposed to inappropriate material. The high level of sexual content on TV, internet and smartphones, along with the male's natural passion for sexual activity leads many young men to "experiment" with sexual content. Don't take it personally if you find your son is struggling notwithstanding all your efforts to protect him and your home.

Young men between 8 and puberty are designed to be curious. They are supposed to explore the world, to be adventurous. According to Freud there is supposed to be a "latency" period around this age. That is a time when sexual things are irrelevant to the young man. This is mostly true, but for an unknown length of time. If the young man comes across pornographic images it will begin the process of argument in his mind. One side of his brain is both curious and stimulated. The other side is disgusted and appalled.

For a parent or a church leader who is discussing pornography or masturbation with a young man, individual discretion is vital. When I am interviewing a young man for the first time, and pornography and/or masturbation are not the main reasons he is coming to see me, I have to ask about them anyway. The presence of such behaviors complicates the therapeutic process for any regular diagnosis. I am usually quite straight forward but vague. "How are you doing with pornography and masturbation?" My tone is clinical and non-judgmental. Before asking such a question, I have already learned a great deal about the young man – especially his strengths, and I have worked to build a relationship of trust and relate ability. After asking the question, I watch their body language closely. If they go quiet, I keep it light and start exploring the extent of the problem. If they answer "no", I will almost always playfully declare them a liar! If the young man has truly been successful, the spirit of the conversation stays warm and playful. If he is lying, he often will become unpleasant and defensive. I try to follow the spirit to decide how much to push. I don't want to destroy the relationship just to find out the truth.

Response to touch – especially in sexual regions.

The memory parts of the brain are especially skilled at documenting any stimulation of the male sex organs. (We use the term [boy parts] to avoid embarrassment for the boys. More official words like "penis" tend to distract the younger boys and the conversation loses its productivity.) This is why boys with a history of being sexually stimulated by adults or other boys have extra challenges as they approach and go through puberty. Most of the Same Sex Attraction boys I have worked with had a very early experience in childhood involving stimulation with another boy/man. A few moments of curiosity with the opposite gender (and similar age) between ages 5 and 10 are not encouraged, but not devastating by any means either.

As boys approach and go through puberty there is a sexual response to just about anything that bumps or brushes against "boy parts". This chemical spill can be very distracting because it takes time (several minutes) for the chemicals to be filtered out of the blood stream, even if they turn their attention to other topics immediately.

Survival of the species – increasing drive to mate with any female within reach.

The animal part of the male brain started to observe a long time ago, that with death and disease, if the human race was going to survive, there needed to be more babies all the time. I believe this is the origin of the male sex drive to "mate with just about anything that walks."

When you combine all of these elements into the untrained mind of a pre-adolescent, it definitely seems like the war is lost before it even begins. Again, by the mercy of God, we have a few resources to our advantage.

Solutions:

Sensitivity – I teach the young men that they have within them something similar to the radar screen of a submarinc. In thc Missionary Training Center, we were taught over and over again, "Help others feel and recognize the Spirit". It took me 2 years to figure out what this meant and begin the process of knowing how to facilitate it. It wasn't until after I learned how these addictions worked that I realized I would also have to teach the young men not only how to feel and recognize the Holy Spirit, but also the spirit of Satan.

Unfortunately, it is easier to teach a young man who has had one or two exposures to pornography how to discern between the spirit of darkness and the spirit of God. I help them remember and feel the spirit of God by having them tell me about a time when they did as vividly as possible. It is not so important that they be able to describe their feelings in words – (such feelings are hard to explain in words, and it can be distracting to try to do so).

First, I have them recall a time and place where they felt the Holy Ghost. I have them remember the location and as much detail as necessary until they re-feel what they had felt at that time. I then encourage them to "book mark" the situation so they can remember how it feels in the future.

I then walk them through the same process when they saw the unfortunate images (or had the experience). Then I have them put the two feelings side by side so that they can compare and contrast them. I try in my own words to give some words that might approximate what the two feelings might be like for them. If it is done right, the young man sharpens his spirit of Discernment.

Warrior Chemistry - boys of all ages tend to have a fascination with things like guns, knives, karate, wrestling, competitive sports, etc. When I work with an individual young man, I try to learn what area he tends to turn to. The male brain is programmed to be skilled at protection. When loved ones are in danger, men will almost universally become ***ferocious*** in defense of the loved one. This ferocity is empowered by a chemical change in the brain and body. We call this Warrior Chemistry.

Most if not all of these young men have already been taught to try to change what they are thinking about when inappropriate thoughts or feelings hit them. They are taught to quote a scripture or sing a hymn. This works fine for a young man who is not yet an addict.

If "deviant chemicals" hit hard enough, at an addict level, the chemicals are going to have to be neutralized in order for the young man to regain control of his mind. He will need to release Warrior Chemistry into his mind before he tries to use his mind for thinking or action.

For a young man who is not yet an addict, the chemicals associated with an intense sporting situation are often sufficient. He will have to practice in order to make it automatic - just like he does in sports or music - with drills, drills and more drills.

"I am afraid to tell my Bishop and/or my parents."

I was pondering what feelings and thoughts a young man is experiencing when he says something like the statement above, when a memory of something I heard several years ago came to my mind. It was a rather disturbing memory, but the more I pondered the similarities, the more accurate it became. It was the memory of something I had learned in another professional setting.

When interviewing children who had experienced unfortunate things at the hands of unfortunate adults, the children said they were told things like...

"Don't tell your parents, or else..."

"You can't tell, because you are the dirty, filthy, child who brought this upon yourself."

"If you hadn't wanted it in the first place, it wouldn't have happened."

"They will reject you for the filth you are if they find out."

As I have interviewed young men who are enslaved by addiction to pornography and masturbation and are afraid to go to their parents or their ecclesiastical leaders for help, I have become more and more confident that there is a Dark Entity like unto a skilled pedophile putting phrases similar to the ones listed into their minds. Satan has had several thousands of years to practice the art and science of doing so. He can make his voice sound just like the voice of the young man. The young man becomes convinced that he is talking to himself.

Most children who have experienced ongoing sexual abuse really do think it is their own fault for some time. In many cases, it is almost impossible to convince them otherwise. It is a very unpleasant dynamic. Satan has a great fear of how important the young man can become if he finds out he is not doing this to himself. You can often measure how much Satan fears a young man by how intense the attacks are.

To the Young Men: Be brave and read closely the lines in italics on the previous page. Now read them as if they are being spoken to one of your little brothers or sisters by a man in a trench coat. How would you feel toward the man in the trench coat? How would you feel toward your younger sibling?

Satan is like the man in the trench coat, except he is meaner and more ruthless. Your brain is like a little brother, young and vulnerable. Your brain is designed to have more than one "voice", and one "voice", when necessary, can protect another. To win the mental battle described above, you must awaken the part of your brain that is naturally conditioned to fight for the protection of women and children. Don't *just* push such thoughts away. You wouldn't just push the man in the trench coat away. You would send an unignorable message that he should never, *ever*, consider messing with you and your loved ones again!

My young Brethren, do not believe the lies you are being told. Run to your parents! Run to your bishop! They love you as you love your younger siblings. They will not consider you to be less than what you are! They understand Satan and will join you in the fight against him. We have found the weapons necessary to beat him and this addiction! It takes training, but it can be done.

If you don't know what to say, just show them this page. It will speak for you. They will rejoice with relief that you asked for help, in the same way you would rejoice with relief if your younger sibling asked you for help.

"When is it Time for Professional Intervention?"

We function on the assumption that parents and ecclesiastical leaders are entitled to revelation on the behalf of each of the young men over whom they have stewardship. In many cases, these stewards obtain sufficient revelation.

A simple, *layman's definition of an addiction* is when will-power is not enough. A simple test can be done to see if the addiction is stronger than the individual's will-power and current relationship with the power of God.

Use your best judgment and revelation to set an achievable goal with the young man. This usually includes:

- Being "perfect" (no pornography and/or masturbation) for a designated time (usually just a few days longer than the recent average number of days of success).
- Committing to and following through on a reading assignment every day during that same time period.

- If the young man fails the first time, set the same type of goals again, but more easily attainable than last time and for a more brief amount of time.
- If the young man succeeds, then, just continue working with him, increasing the commitment line upon line, until he succeeds for a satisfactory length of time.
- If he fails again, let him know that you want to bring out the big guns. Let him know that you want him to get some professional training (not therapy because that word could scare him away) for the specific purpose of overpowering the problem(s). Share with him the confidence you have in the professionals as you feel is appropriate.
- If you predict that he is going to balk at the idea of enrolling in a program, the most effective invitation we have seen starts with, "I want you to check this out." Encourage him (and his parents if he is under 18) to visit with one of our clinicians at least once. Most young men respond well to such a challenge. Our clinicians are specially trained at working with young men with the fears and other emotions associated with these behaviors. They will resolve any concerns and help the young man gain an accurate understanding of what they are up against.

Parent's Appendix

What Can I Do to Help My Son?

I know of few trials more difficult for parents than to discover that their son has a sexual addiction. Sadly, they often will blame themselves for their son's misconduct. This is unfortunate, but there is much that can be done.

First of all, I want to thank you! I have helped many young men overcome addictions in my years as a counselor, but without supportive parents this would not be possible. Some of these loving parents know not what to do other than pick their son up by the shirt collar and drag him to the bishop's office, or to mine. I have watched some sacrifice eating out for therapy sessions, and have done whatever it takes to help their son recover. Thank you for everything you have done and continue to do to help your sons become clean. They will be grateful forever. And, there is a special young woman out there who one day will kneel across a temple altar from your son, giving her whole self over to his protection. She will thank you, her parents will thank you, her children and their children will thank you for helping her husband become a worthy priesthood holder in her home.

In this appendix, I will teach parents about the first steps in helping their sons recover.

Let's start by reviewing an email I received. Perhaps your situation is similar:

Maurice,

My son has a pornography/masturbation problem. He has a strong testimony, but has not been able to take the sacrament for over a year! He started out talking to the bishop once a week, but it slowly became longer and longer between times. And now he hasn't seen him in months. He doesn't like to talk about it with me, and my husband thinks it will just go away. He is 16 1/2 and I don't see how anything is going to change since nothing we have done thus far has helped. Is there any help for him? Can you just help me to know what I should be doing--pressing the issue of counseling or letting it alone. I am very non-judgmental about his situation. I fear for his future and feel like there is no one to talk to about it. Everyone that I can talk to seems to treat it so lightly. My nephew attended your program and it helped him to get on his mission, but I don't want to talk to my sister because I don't want to break a confidence with my son.

Thank you for anything you can help me with.

(Typical Mom)

I wrote the following reply:

Dear Typical Mom,

I feel for your pain. I am sad that you are experiencing this dynamic. We have learned that mothers are the most likely to be strongly invested in getting their sons help. This seems to be for two reasons.

First, it is true that some fathers have a tendency to down play it. Mostly because men don't want to insult their son's confidence by telling them, "You aren't capable of fixing this on your own." Instinctually, the father remembers that one of the most important emotional experiences to have as a young man is the acquisition of confidence; the, "I can do anything I put my mind to" sensation. Also, in many cases with fathers when they were young men, the behavior(s) never hit the addict level. If the father never became an addict, then will-power would have been enough to overcome the "bad habit". Unfortunately, it appears that your son has reached the addict level - where willpower is not enough.

Second, the strong mother instinct to make sure her children are prepared for adult life is burning strong inside of you. Part of your responsibility is to feel what it is going to be like to be a wife to this young man. You, 10 times more than either your husband or your Bishop, know how much pain it is going to cause your son's wife if he doesn't overpower this addiction before he is married. Also, you are guessing with decent accuracy how he is going to feel if he is unable to serve a mission or has it significantly delayed. Finally, you sense what years of "lost battles" will do to his confidence if he doesn't acquire the needed training to win the war.

Almost every Bishop I have worked with has great intent and works hard. Their responsibilities are broad and deep. I would not be surprised if the Bishop has gotten overwhelmed with other things and your son has accidentally fallen through the cracks. I have recommended to other mothers in this situation to make their own appointment with the Bishop and remind him of your concerns. The Bishop should be able to call your son in for a visit without revealing that you have spoken to him.

In the past, I have run your question, "What should I do as a mother?" past my groups of young men and have gotten some interesting responses. Most of them sound something like, "Knock the kid over the head, drag him in here, throw him on the couch and let him wake up in the middle of a group session. He will be grateful for the rest of his life." This may be a little extreme, but the young men agree, once you get past the initial embarrassment (first 5 minutes) the experience of seeing real, quality young men, fighting shoulder to shoulder against a ferocious enemy, they build skills and brotherhood to last a lifetime.

In real life application, contact our office for two reasons. One, the office manager can refer you to other mothers who are willing to talk to new mothers to help resolve concerns and give ideas. Two, set an appointment to meet with one of our clinicians. Get the direct phone number for the clinician in order to discuss the situation with him so he can help guide you through the specifics on how to help your son get in for an assessment - to see if the problem is bad enough to warrant professional help. The clinician will recommend something like the following depending on the hypersensitivity of your son. Before leaving for the appointment, tell your son, "I have someone I want you to meet." On the way there say, "I was reading about a special training program for young men, and I wanted us both to meet with these people to see if it would be a good idea to follow through on." Our clinicians are very experienced and well trained to handle this sensitive transition. In almost every case, once the young man meets the clinician, everything flows. If the clinician recommends something less than Sons of Helaman, you can have confidence in his recommendations.

Finally, do not take it too personally that your son is not confiding in you. This is almost universal. In two ways it is actually a good sign, developmentally. One, it means your son has a respect for you as a woman and does not want to contaminate you with the problem. Second, he is trying to complete his sense of "Competency" development....he wants to prove that he can do something without help. Part of what we train the young men is that "lost battles" are not a sign of weakness, but a sign of how big of an army Satan is sending against you because he is afraid of what you will become as a full grown man! We follow that by teaching him that no intelligent military strategist would send one warrior alone against such a large army. This helps him maintain self-value and get help at the same time.

There is hope. Your son can overcome his addiction. "[He] can do all things through Christ, which strengtheneth [him]" (Philippians 4:13).

The Sons of Helaman Program
And Your Son

For many years, *Sons of Helaman* has been working to perfect the Spiritual Warfare techniques that are needed to beat pornography/masturbation addiction for a lifetime. During this time, participants and clinicians alike have come to realize the crucial role that an addict's family, especially his parents, can play in his life-long victory over this demon that assails him.

Often, as a parent, you may feel powerless and clueless when it comes to helping your son. First, realize that **this is a battle your <u>son</u> has to fight**; unfortunately you cannot take away the pain or his responsibility. Second, just as the Sons of Helaman in the *Book of Mormon* benefitted and were inspired by the love and support their parents showed, your son's progress can be greatly helped as you *plan with him* how to best support him.

Parent's Dos

Most of the following were created by the young men of Sons of Helaman.

Do:

- Involve both parents; mothers or fathers should not be alone in the support of their son.
- Read this book, *Like Dragons Did They Fight.*
- Find ways your son can work in exchange for program payment.
- Read the Green Book, *Putting on the Armor of God,* by Steven Cramer.
- Plan with your boy your level of support and involvement. It will change as he progresses.
- Attend the monthly Parents' Meeting of the Sons of Helaman™ Program.
- Ask "Are you pleased with your progress?" but don't always wait for an answer.
- Help me get new ideas to help me win. Ask if I want them before you give them
- Let me know how proud you are of me. Watch my calendar and cheer me on every time I succeed.
- Express confidence in me and give me encouragement.
- Remember, I am still your son and I am doing my best.
- Pray for me.
- Be sensitive to my mood shifts (they are often associated with difficult battles).
- Sit down with me and outline do's and don'ts (for those under 18).
- Help when I ask for it. Help in the way that I ask you to help me.
- If I ask for something unusual, be supportive – ask my therapist if you are concerned.
- Talk to me, but LISTEN – I will try to tell you the truth, but sometimes I don't even know what is going on.

- Get advice from the therapist that runs my group- don't be afraid to talk to him.
- Offer Father's blessings- Often!
- Come to me to offer help; don't wait for me to come to you.
- Check on me every day (but not more than twice a day unless I ask for it). But don't lecture me every day.
- Learn about the addiction. Learn about the Satanic Spin. Look for deeper reasons why I am an addict.
- Understand how addicting and painful this can be for me and be there for me.
- Discuss with me and remind me why I am being attacked – because I am a threat to Satan – point out specific reasons why Satan would fear me.
- Use Positive Assumption Reminders: "You have probably already remembered to do your Border Patrol"; "You probably already remembered to mark your calendar."
- Set family rewards for progress. Put my "MAN PoWeR Calendar" on the refrigerator and suggest the whole family get a reward if there are positive points or a perfect week. (This should only be done with young man's approval.)
- Express worry about the pain (both current and future) but not about my ability to win. When expressing concerns, never attack my character.
- Remember, I am not the enemy. Remember, it is you and me against a 7,000 year old genius.
- I want your help, but not if you make me feel stupid or weak. That doesn't help.

Parent's Don'ts

Most of the following were created by the young men of Sons of Helaman.

"Mom and Dad, please don't..."

- Ridicule.
- Be sarcastic.
- Stop caring.
- Impose your goals on me; let me set the goals then find out how you can help me achieve them. I will increase them as we go. It scares me to set goals that feel unachievable right now.
- Get angry. It is okay for moms to get scared. A mom's response should be similar to how she thinks a young bride would respond.
- Be uninvolved.
- Feel bad that this is a war Satan has chosen for me. I am a threat to Satan. What were you expecting was going to happen? Did you think he would leave someone as awesome as me alone?
- Persistently ask me how I am doing when friends or family are over. It is embarrassing.
- Tell me you are disappointed in *me* – rather focus on my actions/behaviors.
- Interrupt me when I am doing Border Patrol.
- Blame yourself.
- Feel like it is your fault, because it isn't.
- *For Dads*: Don't keep an addiction you may have from your son. He needs to hear it from you. He will figure it out eventually anyway. He needs to know how you beat it, or that you are working with sweat and blood to do so.
- Punish me for "lost battles" – I am already punishing myself.
- Talk about the problem so much that it becomes annoying (set time intervals, determined by when I would like you to check up on me).
- Freak out when I am brave enough to confide in you.
- Scream or yell.

- Try to control the problem. Instead, just listen and help me come up with a plan.
- Broadcast my problem. Don't let the secret out.
- Be on my back about it, but be there when I need you.
- Run away from the problem, the problem will not fix itself.
- **Don't give up on me!**

Bishop's Appendix

(As a reminder, while this author has worked hard to make sure the information in this book correlates with the teachings of the LDS Church in order to specifically serve that population; this work is not an official publication of The Church of Jesus Christ of Latter-day Saints. The views expressed herein are the responsibility of the author and do not necessarily represent the position of the Church.)

How do I Help this Young Man?

Many bishops and other church leaders who counsel with men who are facing pornography and/or masturbation addiction often wonder what to do for these men and their families. Any addiction has a physical as well as a spiritual component. In the years that our therapists have been helping individuals access the tools they need for success, we have found it useful to understand both the spiritual and physical side of addiction and how they interact.

The following is to help you, as a bishop, add to the knowledge, wisdom, and resources you already have in this battle.

Addict or Experimenter?

Bishops have done a wonderful job at helping young men who have occasional "run ins" with unwanted sexual addiction behaviors. Usually in this case, a few meetings with the bishop and a commitment from the young man can take care of the problem on their own. Unfortunately, when the problem gets to be a chronic and consuming encounter for the young man, he needs to see a professional if he is to get the tools that he needs to get the problem under control. The simplest way to define an addict is if he can't keep his promises - even to himself. When he first informs you of the problem, let him know that you have three things that you want to try. First, create a contract with him based on your own inspiration. **Give him a list of 'to-dos' and 'not-to-dos'**. Check back with him in a week. **If he can't keep these promises twice**—you can inform him that he is possibly an addict and that you want him to try out some professional training. **If he succeeds with your ideas**—just keep working with him till he has things under control.

The Options

As mentioned above, when an individual is not able to keep promises regarding their behavior, they are in need of some outside help. This book is not a comprehensive resource, but rather, an overview of the resources that are available for addressing addictions. No one form of treatment has the corner on the market for effectiveness. Much of the success of an individual depends on how well the treatment option fits their situation and personality.

Option 1: *Meet with the Bishop*. Many young men find it intimidating and scary to go from the Bishop's office to a stranger's office. They may feel shame or embarrassment. In cases where the young man does not want to see a professional, you may want to continue meeting with him regularly, setting small, obtainable goals to help him progress. Some young men take time to warm up to the idea of seeing a professional, occasionally remind him that there are people who have dealt with this issue before and who have tools that he may find useful.

Option 2: *Individual Therapy*. The individual will meet with a therapist (a master's or doctoral level professional who has been trained in one-on-one counseling). A session is generally about an hour long and the frequency is determined by the therapist and the individual receiving services. The content of the meetings will depend on the therapist's background and specialty. This option provides in-depth analysis and treatment of the addiction. It is expensive and progress can be slower than other options because the young warrior still feels like he is the only one with the problem.

Sons of Helaman has many qualified clinicians that can provide good one-on-one care for this issue and is a good place to start in finding a clinician who can help your ward members with any issue. LDS Family Services has good clinicians as well if there are no Sons of Helaman clinicians nearby.

Option 3: ***Support Groups***. These groups are a collection of individuals who have similar experience and can provide support, encouragement, and some insight to each other. Support groups are not run by therapists. The Church's Twelve Step Program is a support group. Couple missionaries provide the staffing for them and are there to encourage and moderate the discussion, sometimes educating on specific, related topics. While support groups do not provide the same in-depth treatment that therapy does, they provide good support. Many therapists recommend that their clients who are dealing with sexual addiction attend support groups in addition to therapy for "extra help". Any kind of group approach is much more cost-effective than individual therapy. Support groups are generally free or have minimal cost. How often one attends a support group is completely up the individual.

Option 4: *Training Groups*. This is a step between support groups and therapy groups. I wanted to find a bridge for those who needed something more intense than a support group, but didn't have the finances to pay for group therapy. These groups are run in a classroom type setting where confrontation between participants and accountability is expected. Training groups have proven to be very powerful.

Option 5: *Group Therapy*. This option combines the best of both worlds. In group therapy, a licensed therapist facilitates discussion while providing in-depth treatment to an individual. Group therapy has the effect of an individual receiving "higher doses" of treatment when compared to individual therapy. Because multiple people attend and work on issues, it is like having multiple individual sessions all at once. Group therapy costs considerably less than individual therapy, and tends to a get results faster. It is usually a less intimidating option than individual therapy and is effective at reducing shame, a critical part of any kind of addiction treatment. In most cases, professionals prefer group therapy to other treatment options for addiction.

The Sons of Helaman program was designed to provide a more cost-effective, enjoyable, and powerful way to address pornography and/or masturbation addiction in young men who are preparing for their missions or the temple. The young men find the group therapy setting to be ideal for teaching the skills that are needed to win this battle for a lifetime.

Getting from the Bishop's Office To the Therapist's Office

Most young men recoil at the thought of "going to therapy"; it sounds scary, and makes them feel like their problem is much bigger than they can deal with. In the event that you feel the young man needs to see a professional, take the following steps. Inform the young man that you 'know some people'—some "experts that have dealt with this issue and they have some tools that might benefit him that you, the Bishop, do not have." Nobody likes to be 'enrolled' in a program. That makes them nervous. Commit the boy and/or his parents (if they are already informed of the problem, and if you feel it is appropriate) to "**just check it out**. If it isn't going to work for you, then don't worry about it."

In the case of the Sons of Helaman program, you can share with him the appropriate information- a pamphlet, or refer him to our website **www.sonsofhelaman.org.** If he might drop the ball, we can make the initial call to him after you supply us with his number.

The hardest part in the whole process is making the first call. Patiently encourage the young man and/or his parents.

Some boys and parents are more comfortable receiving a call from a professional rather than trying to build up the courage to call themselves. With their permission, you can pass their information along and tell them to expect a call. Once they get over that initial fear and an intake interview, attending a group where they will find peers and tools that will help them to win is only a matter of time.

Another idea that has worked with modern technology: after discussing the need and finding the young man is still "on the fence". Ask to borrow his cell phone, then text "Help" to 91011, and we will take it from there. It is a little forward, but most young men appreciate it afterward.

Bishop's Dos

Most of the following were created by the young men of Sons of Helaman.

Do:

- Involve both parents, if the young man wants them to know about the issue. Mothers or fathers should not be alone in the support of their son. The more support a young man has, the more chance he has at defeating the addiction.
- Read this book, *Like Dragons Did They Fight*. Learn how a spiritual warrior has to think and feel to beat this addiction. Your insights into Satan's strategies and the Lord's weapons can make a big difference for a young man.
- Find ways your boy can work in exchange for program payment (if the ward is paying for his visits).
- Read the Green Book, *Putting on the Armor of God*, by Steven Cramer
- Plan with your boy your level of support and involvement; some Bishops have short phone calls several times a week to provide encouragement and accountability. Texting is pretty powerful.
- Ask a Sons of Helaman Clinician to visit your ward to train you and your members to more effectively fight this battle. There are many fronts to this battle. Mothers, fathers, girlfriends, and the boys themselves all need specialized training on the issue.
- Help him get new ideas to help him win (as a Bishop, you are a key player in the success and spiritual strength of a young man who has come to you, he needs your insight).
- Pray for him.
- Talk to him, but LISTEN. He will try to tell you the truth, but sometimes he won't even know what is going on (Reading 'the Green Book' will help you to understand these instances when a young man is confused about what is going on).
- Offer Priesthood blessings- Often!

- Check on him frequently (many of the boys who are successful meet with their Bishops *at least* on a monthly basis).
- Learn about the addiction. Learn about the cycle. Look for deeper reasons why he is an addict.
- Discuss with him and remind him why he is being attacked – because he is a threat to Satan – point out specific reasons why Satan would fear him.
- Ask the young man to bring his progress calendar to your meetings with him.
- Set worthiness goals with the young man: when he can fill out mission papers, pass the sacrament, advance in the priesthood. As far as we know, there are no church-wide standards on this. Counsel with the young man to determine how many perfect weeks he should have before he can expect to be considered for the above.

Bishop's Don'ts

Most of the following were created by the young men of Sons of Helaman.

"Bishop, Please Don't:"

- Stop caring. Even a boy who has stopped coming to church and meeting with you will appreciate occasional calls or visits to see how he is doing.
- Impose your goals. Let him set the goals and find out how you can help him achieve them.
- Minimize or maximize the problem. It takes a lot for a boy to come to his Bishop with this set of issues. While it is serious and potentially very damaging, don't make the boy feel like it is the end of the world. At the same time, don't minimize the seriousness. Many boys feel relieved to come to a group and see so many other good young men struggling with the same issue. Let the boy know he is not alone and that there are many people who have also overcome this addiction with the right tools.
- Punish me for "lost battles" – This doesn't include withholding the privilege of participating in Priesthood ordinances. Help the young man understand the importance of worthiness so he doesn't see such exclusion as a punishment.
- Try to control the problem, talk about it, and just listen. Help me come up with a plan (see *Addict or Experimenter* section).
- Be afraid to request more contact from the therapist- we are trying to facilitate frequent contact, but it is a big job. Our therapists are more than happy to talk to you about your boy's progress.

Suggested Readings

Putting on the Armor of God, by Steven Cramer (the Green Book)

Will Power is not Enough, by Byrd and Chamberlain

Outwitting the Devil, by Napoleon Hill

The Screwtape Letters, by C.S. Lewis

As a Man Thinketh, by James Allen

Wild at Heart, by John Eldridge

"Winning the War against Evil," by James J. Hamula, *General Conference, Priesthood Session,* October 2008

"Happiness, Your Heritage," by President Dieter F. Uchtdorf, *General Relief Society Meeting,* September 2008

The war chapters of the Book of Mormon, for an insight into what your young man might be feeling as a warrior, and the supportive role of families

"Man Down!" by President Henry B. Eyring, *General Conference, Priesthood Session,* April 2009

"We Are All Enlisted," by Jeffrey R. Holland, *General Conference, Priesthood Session,* October 2011

GiRL PoWeR Calendar

G ____________________ P ____________________

R ____________________ W ____________________

L ____________________ R ____________________

Date	Day:		Date	Day:		Date	Day:		Date	Day:		Date	Day:		Date	Day:		Date	Day:	
G	R	L	G	R	L	G	R	L	G	R	L	G	R	L	G	R	L	G	R	L
P	W	R	P	W	R	P	W	R	P	W	R	P	W	R	P	W	R	P	W	R
Date	Day:		Date	Day:		Date	Day:		Date	Day:		Date	Day:		Date	Day:		Date	Day:	
G	R	L	G	R	L	G	R	L	G	R	L	G	R	L	G	R	L	G	R	L
P	W	R	P	W	R	P	W	R	P	W	R	P	W	R	P	W	R	P	W	R
Date	Day:		Date	Day:		Date	Day:		Date	Day:		Date	Day:		Date	Day:		Date	Day:	
G	R	L	G	R	L	G	R	L	G	R	L	G	R	L	G	R	L	G	R	L
P	W	R	P	W	R	P	W	R	P	W	R	P	W	R	P	W	R	P	W	R
Date	Day:		Date	Day:		Date	Day:		Date	Day:		Date	Day:		Date	Day:		Date	Day:	
G	R	L	G	R	L	G	R	L	G	R	L	G	R	L	G	R	L	G	R	L
P	W	R	P	W	R	P	W	R	P	W	R	P	W	R	P	W	R	P	W	R
Date	Day:		Date	Day:		Date	Day:		Date	Day:		Date	Day:		Date	Day:		Date	Day:	
G	R	L	G	R	L	G	R	L	G	R	L	G	R	L	G	R	L	G	R	L
P	W	R	P	W	R	P	W	R	P	W	R	P	W	R	P	W	R	P	W	R

MAN PoWeR Calendar

M		P	
A		W	
N		R	

Date	Day:		Date	Day:		Date	Day:		Date	Day:		Date	Day:		Date	Day:		Date	Day:	
M	A	N	M	A	N	M	A	N	M	A	N	M	A	N	M	A	N	M	A	N
P	W	R	P	W	R	P	W	R	P	W	R	P	W	R	P	W	R	P	W	R
Date	Day:		Date	Day:		Date	Day:		Date	Day:		Date	Day:		Date	Day:		Date	Day:	
M	A	N	M	A	N	M	A	N	M	A	N	M	A	N	M	A	N	M	A	N
P	W	R	P	W	R	P	W	R	P	W	R	P	W	R	P	W	R	P	W	R
Date	Day:		Date	Day:		Date	Day:		Date	Day:		Date	Day:		Date	Day:		Date	Day:	
M	A	N	M	A	N	M	A	N	M	A	N	M	A	N	M	A	N	M	A	N
P	W	R	P	W	R	P	W	R	P	W	R	P	W	R	P	W	R	P	W	R
Date	Day:		Date	Day:		Date	Day:		Date	Day:		Date	Day:		Date	Day:		Date	Day:	
M	A	N	M	A	N	M	A	N	M	A	N	M	A	N	M	A	N	M	A	N
P	W	R	P	W	R	P	W	R	P	W	R	P	W	R	P	W	R	P	W	R
Date	Day:		Date	Day:		Date	Day:		Date	Day:		Date	Day:		Date	Day:		Date	Day:	
M	A	N	M	A	N	M	A	N	M	A	N	M	A	N	M	A	N	M	A	N
P	W	R	P	W	R	P	W	R	P	W	R	P	W	R	P	W	R	P	W	R

MAN/GRL PoWeR CALENDAR INSTRUCTIONS

Using the MAN/GiRL PoWeR Calendar is a training tool designed to instill within your mind and spirit the power and weapons needed to override temptations and possible addictions. Before now, you can probably identify times when your moods/feelings have overpowered your values (i.e., "I value getting out of bed on time, but I don't feel like it."). This pattern just happens to be the most common decision making pattern that makes a person susceptible to addictions i.e., "I value avoiding drugs/alcohol/pornography, but I don't feel like controlling myself right now." The more frequently you make decisions this way, the more likely you are to fall to temptation and/or addiction when the opportunity presents itself.

By using this calendar, you will strengthen your ability to have your values overpower your moods i.e., "I value getting out of bed on time, and no matter how I feel, or what my mood is, I will do so." By the time you master 28 days of using your calendar, you will be able to follow through on the things you really care about i.e., "I value eating in a healthy way, and I can make myself do so no matter how I feel."

To begin, you must choose three target ***Behaviors*** that you want to perfect. You will also be working to perfect three daily ***Actions*** that will be necessary to strengthen your mind and spirit to win against the attacks of Satan. We call these six things "MAN PoWeR".

Feel free to look at the list of ideas that follow, or choose your own. Keeping the calendar is designed to be on-going. In other words, once you have perfected your three target behaviors you can choose three new target behaviors.

You will record your won and lost battles on this calendar. In order for a day to count as a "perfect" day, you must succeed in all three MAN target behaviors, and all three PoWeR actions on that day. At the end of 28 perfect days, feel free to set new goals. If you do not have a "perfect" day, you start over at day one. Yes, this is true also for those who get to 27 days!

PoWeR Actions

PoWeR actions are the three most powerful daily activities you can be doing in order to be prepared to fight off temptation and addiction. You will probably recognize them. You will need to customize each for yourself, but you need to get to the point where you can at least do the minimum in each category every day.

- P=Prayer: Connect with God in a meaningful way. Approximately 5 min, twice a day.
- W=Write: a letter to God and/or to Future Spouse every day. Be accountable. Make promises. Discuss strategies and motives.
- R =Read: At least ___ min/day, words of the prophets and other inspired authors.

MAN/GRL Squares

"And Jesus increased in wisdom and stature and in favour with God and man." (Luke 2:52)

From this scripture we learn that Jesus grew in four specific areas: intellectual, physical, spiritual and social/emotional. This is a good guideline for goal setting. We call these P.I.E.S. goals.

Here are some P.I.E.S. ideas for your MAN/GRL behaviors:

Physical
- Out of bed on time
- Exercise
- Eat Healthier

Intellectual
- Memorizing scriptures
- Reading inspiring books

Emotional/Social
- Get to school/appointments and meetings on time
- Do something every day that will maintain an edifying relationship with family members
- Regulate emotional responses
- At least one spontaneous act of service

Spiritual- these will be your PoWeR actions

- P=Prayer: At least 5 min twice a day
- W=Write: A letter to God and/or to future spouse every day
- R=Read: At least 30 min/day, words of the prophets, ancient and/or modern. Read 2 pages from *Like Dragons Did They Fight*

Your goals need to be clearly articulated. They need to be specific, measurable, attainable, and realistic, and have a time in which to complete them. For example, if my goal is to get up early enough to exercise and still be ready for school on time, I might set goals that read like this:

I exercise thirty minutes a day. I get out of bed at 6:00 a.m. five days a week. My choices of exercise include stretches, kick boxing or strength training.

More Ideas:
Out of bed on time without help
Get to school/meetings/events without help
Get homework done and turned in without reminders
Get family contribution activities (chores) done without reminders
Treat adults (especially parents) with respect in all situations
Get to bed on time
At least one spontaneous act of service
Edifying relations with siblings
Controlled use of video games
Controlled use of Social media
No drug use
No alcohol use
No pornography or masturbation
No morality issues
No self-harm behaviors